THE N FACTOR

THE N FACTOR

How Efficient Networking Can
Change the Dynamics of Your
Business

Written by
Adrie Reinders & Marion Freijsen

W Business
Books

an imprint of New Win Publishing
a division of Academic Learning Company, LLC

Library of Congress Cataloging-in-Publication Data

Reinders, Adrie.
  The N factor : how efficient networking can change the dynamics of your
business / Adrie Reinders, Marion Freijsen.
     p. cm.
  ISBN 0-8329-5006-8 (hardcover)
  1. Business networks. 2. Interpersonal communication. I. Freijsen, Marion.
II. Title.
HD69.S8R447 2007
658'.044–dc22

                                    2006039256

"No man is an island entire unto itself."
—John Donne

Thanks to the N Factor approach, I was able to find my brother after more than 50 years.

—Adrie Reinders

Contents

Prologue

During the greatest part of my life I have been a technology entrepreneur. Envisioning concepts and acting to make them a reality is what I enjoy most. However, building a company is not something done in isolation. True success depends on an ongoing liaison with many, thus building upon one's knowledge base. To develop a universe of other professionals with whom to collaborate - is an art, the art of networking.

It is a given that developing and managing productive relationships with a diverse audience is the basis for a successful operation. Equity holders, directors, employees, customers, suppliers of goods and services et al, all contribute to a firm's viability.

Experience has taught me that productive dealings, especially with the right people, result in business success. You establish professional relationships, a network upon which one can rely in a multitude of circumstances, maybe even "to fall back on" to. Only in the recent past have I realized that networking is truly an art.

Thus I became increasingly interested in this unique professional phenomenon of networking. I was doing a lot of it but not as well as I could have done. This resulted ultimately in the realization that maintenance of what, for me, had become a large network required structure, management and organization, lest its benefit be lost. There were valuable lessons to learn along the way. And, as Confucius taught, I would like to share what I have gained. This book, therefore, aims to pass on to you my perspective on one of the most essential elements of business transactions and interaction. Confucius instructs us that each individual is obliged to perform as best as they can in whatever they choose to do and ensure their knowledge and skills are passed on to those who come after. This ideal inspired me to write this book and share the valuable lessons of starting, building, and managing a successful network.

I am very fortunate to have worked in an age that is open to enterprise, in an industry that defines innovation and to have come from a country acknowledged as free, open and entrepreneurial. The same spirit attracted me to the U.S. where we established a base in the early eighties. However, given the common universe of business ethics and the rules of human interaction, where you are or where you work are subordinate to respect and openness for cultures and practices other than your own.

Introduction

This book has been written with two groups of people in mind: the High Potential and the Starting Entrepreneur.

If you are either, it could be that you do not yet realize that ultimate success in your career or business depends to a large degree on how successful you are in creating your own network.

Creating a network is a profession within a profession and needs to be structured well. It requires an ongoing active investment in time, taking many years to build. It will however offer you a greater return as time goes on.

The so-called High Potentials are young, well-educated people, late twenties to late thirties, working for large organizations. This group has the advantage of being introduced to technology from an early age and is used to living in a "virtual" world. As a High Potential you have your career mapped out in front of you. You have been selected by large organizations such as Unilever or Shell to follow a management program, exposing you to a variety of business areas and teaching you various skills with the sole purpose for you to achieve a senior position in the organization at some future point in your career.

The second group, Starting Entrepreneurs, whether younger or older, have a number of things in common: they are creative, "stubborn" in their views, strongly motivated, and very focused on realizing their ambition to distribute their service or product via their very own organization. They are impatient for success, looking for a quick win. However, this is contradictory to the fact that a network takes time to build, an investment that you make over time. You may already network a bit, intuitively (as you will have been forced to do from the day you started your own business) but often the danger is that you seek quantity instead of quality.

The common factor between these two groups is that they will need a network to achieve their ambition.

So what is the issue with these groups?

Entrepreneurs

This book is written with entrepreneurs in mind. In my view, entrepreneurs are a special type: they will often leave school early; they are not at their best in larger organizations and therefore are not easy to manage; and they voice their opinions clearly and have a mind of their own. If I look back on my own early career, working for smaller or larger organizations, things often started going wrong because I viewed the management team and business models with a critical eye. And often, I would not hide my views. However, my criticisms, suggestions and ideas would be discarded by my managers. If you are in the middle of this, you have the feeling you are "different." You don't quite fit in. And there is always a dream in the back of your mind to start out on your own, to do things differently. And what you see then, is that a lot of other people have the same drive and that there are a number of things these people have in common.

They have a dream

They have an enormous drive

They want to win

And mostly, against all advice, they continue to believe in their mission.

The catalyst can sometimes be technology, other times it can be sales. In all cases, there is the will to succeed. It does not really matter where you are an entrepreneur – be it Europe, the U.S. or Israel. You do see however, that because of the increased popularity of Initial Public Offerings (IPOs), there are a large number of entrepreneurs who are driven solely by expected financial gain. This is the case in particular in the U.S. and Israel. If you observe Silicon Valley where around 10,000 technology companies are currently operating and where there is a huge pool of talent and money, the founding of a company has almost become an academic exercise. First comes the idea, then angel financing, next comes product development. After a couple of years there's financing by a professional institution such as venture capitalist or financial, then taking the product to the market and after five to seven years realizing a merger or IPO.

In such an almost scientifically prepared process, it is of incredible importance to have or build a sound network. Your network is one of the most critical success factors. We call this the N Factor.

The N Factor is not only about finding talent, angel financing and knowing the right venture capitalists, most of all, it is about creating an exit and knowing the right people who can help you shorten the lead time in the sales trajectory. Because you know people, they will help you get to where you need or want to be. In short, they emphasize and lend you the credibility to realize your success.

From my own experience, I know that entrepreneurs are not the most likely people to work systematically at their networks nor to register and manage their networks. They often do this "as it happens." As the N Factor is of critical importance to the success of every organization, I will provide you with a number of examples in this book from creation via expansion to structuring of your network.

High Potentials

As High Potentials you often have relatively easy access through your organization to external contacts. This may create the false impression that proactive networking is not necessary or even that networking itself is very easy. You may fail to realize that the apparent simplicity of making contact is based on the strength of your company's brand or the product you represent. As a High Potential of a large organization such as Procter & Gamble you will of course be received more easily into a circle, than if you were approaching the same circle as Joe or Jane Blogs of Blogs & Partners Inc.

It is easy as a High Potential to neglect to see that while you are well-educated and receive special attention in your own organization—courses and programs especially geared towards you—an internal network is almost of equal importance as an external one. Moreover, it is also imperative to have a group around you that will support you on your way up.

One of my early and wise employers used to say to me: "If you ever do end up working in a large organization, make sure you get noticed. If that means you have to quarrel or argue with your bosses, do so. There is nothing more deadly to your career than having been working for a company for over ten years, and nobody even knows you."

Throughout your career, you will equally need your network to help you reach decisions and achieve your goals. If you don't have such a group around you, you will be blindfolded as you go. You will need to have access to all layers of your organization. For instance, it may be helpful to have access to a former teammate who is now the manager in Bangladesh who will be able to supply you with local information that could prove invaluable to you.

High Potentials are often found in the age-group of thirty to forty. With a short period of working experience behind you, you now reach the most critical, defining period of your careers. Having enjoyed a sound education, you may have commenced working at around twenty-five years of age – often starting in the lower ranks of a large organization. This organization will typically have a hierarchical structure based on the shape of a pyramid. As you look up, the tip of the pyramid is hiding in clouds and although you know that you want to move up the ladder, it is not clear yet how far you may rise and exactly how many others are climbing the same path. Moreover, one must realize that there is only a limited time in which you can still make it to the top. If you don't get to the higher echelons of your organization by the time you are forty-five, you can safely assume you will never make it all the way up the pyramid either. In short, there are about fifteen to twenty years if you are lucky to take the steps you need to get there, so why not use all the help you can. A network will most certainly give you a competitive advantage.

The era of life-time employment is history. It may seem, when working for a large organization and being recognized as a High Potential that the world is at your feet and you are assured of a solid career at that organization. However, history has proven that this is definitely not always the case. In this time of shareholders' value, the key goal of the organization is profitability. We have clearly seen in the past decade that this is often achieved by Cost Savings which in turn has led to a large number of Mergers & Acquisitions. Whole industries are being consolidated – banking, telecommunications, even the steel industry; nothing escapes the M&A rush. This leads to thousands of job losses as companies are brought together. So what happens now? You happen to be part of the wrong side; tough luck but you are no longer required as part of the core team. You will have to look for another position...so who do you know?

As an entrepreneur you have a totally different problem. Often you will have to manage so many different things at the same time. You will be working at all times and you may think you do not have the time to establish a network. You feel you are not able to spare time to go to meetings, events or professional gatherings let alone find time to go play a round of golf or visit a concert with a group of professionals or a summer BBQ. Before you know it, you become isolated and find the world is passing you by.

Another issue facing entrepreneurs is the fact that there is often a limited window of opportunity to market your product or service and equally often, a limited amount of cash available. As an entrepreneur you will have to find ways to speed up the process of going to market. You cannot afford to lose a lot of time.

Other aspects that lead to the time-pressure High Potentials and entrepreneurs face today is the changing demographics. While (mostly) men used to be able to build their careers and their spouses ran their homes and eased pressure from this side – these days, often both partners are working simultaneously on their careers. They therefore have to juggle the pressures of work and family. This professional couple will probably decide to postpone having children until they are in their mid-thirties due to their career plans. The result is two High Potentials juggling the need to work long hours and finding time for their family and themselves. This time restraint would limit them to accept invitations or invest time in building other relationships no matter how crucial these may be to their careers. It becomes all too easy to see "social" gatherings as merely "fun" and something that can be done without as opposed to an item that forms a highly critical element of their future success.

In a world where quantitative skills and analysis have been emphasized over qualitative abilities at every turn of the road, High Potentials and entrepreneurs alike may well believe that eventually all decisions will be made in a purely analytical quantitative framework and thus negate the need for a relationship with the decision maker.

However, given it is more likely than ever that in any opportunity there are likely to be several products, services, or individuals that are equally capable of delivering the desired outcome, it seems that the strength of the relationship and the network may be the final deciding factor in such instances.

Why The N Factor?

To understand what you are trying to achieve, you have to know what we mean when we use the N for Networking.

As we see it, networking is:

Building and maintaining relationships to establish a trust basis for the long term.

Networking is something that you should start doing the moment you enter the business world. Unfortunately, instead of it being a conscious process, it is often something that people have unconsciously and haphazardly done during their careers.

Nowadays, technology plays a key role in all fields. As we perceive the world getting smaller and smaller, the rapid growth in competition in whichever field you choose to be in becomes evident. Therefore, it is essential to create a competitive advantage for yourselves. Business is essentially all about dealing with people. That is exactly why you have to know them.

Let's take a few examples:

Time to Market

It is not only a matter of development time; it is also a matter of traction in the market. You need to know people in order to get in front of the right person quickly.

Local Knowledge

When you expand your business to other geographies or countries you have to rely on people you know and trust to provide you with relevant information about the area you are moving into and its culture. These individuals can also help you when things get tough.

Internal Networking

For those of you in a large organization, a network is an absolute must at all levels.

Employment

At the point in time you have to look for alternative employment, building relationships is too late. It is reported that at least 60 percent * —some say even higher—of all jobs are found by networking. Of course the opposite is also true, when looking for new people for your business you can use your network to find people you can rely on.

Financing/Mergers & Acquisitions (M&A)

For fund-raising it is absolutely essential to know who

* Source from www.linkedin.com/.

provides your money. They should suit your business and add real value to it. They should not take ages in coming to a decision. For Financing, trust is the vital ingredient.

With regards to M&A, trust is even more important. If you are being acquired, it usually only happens once. It is therefore a key decision you will make in your business's life. Often your payment will be structured by way of an "earn-out" or with shares in the acquiring company. If it goes wrong – there is no way back. Therefore, the views of people you know and trust can provide valuable insights on the acquiring company or even, in the best case scenario, they could introduce the acquirer to you.

With a merger – due diligence can tell you a lot about a company, but it tells very little about the key people you will have to deal with. And yet, in more than 50 percent of the problem cases, this is exactly where it all goes wrong.

Large organizations are often also multinational organizations. It is highly likely that you will end up overseas for at least a period of time. This is a unique opportunity to learn another culture, to work with a different nationality and learn to manage both cultures in a work environment. Don't be tempted to stay within your own nationality regardless of the many groups you get invited to join. Use your time wisely and you will reap the benefits later on. When you do spend time abroad, it is always worthwhile getting to know local governments and visit Chambers of Commerce as these can be very helpful in getting to know others. This can benefit you if you should want to establish a base here at a future time.

Often people think of networking as a technique for selling goods, services, and/or brands more easily. However, there are a number of other good reasons why a strong network can be critical to your business.

For instance, in 1989 I founded Rijnhaave, a technology company. From the early days, the strategy was based on doing a roll-up with acquisitions in a number of European countries and the U.S. This would provide the basis on which we could continue to build the company organically. However, at the most critical moment—the consolidation phase of the acquired companies—the world hit an economic downturn. Information Technology, our market segment, was especially hard hit. This caused a number of financial institutions who were involved with Rijnhaave, to revoke their lines of credit. Without my network, this would have been the end of the organization. The company teetered on the edge of collapse. At such times, you truly experience the benefits of a strong network. In a very short time-span, I was able to mobilize accountants, shareholders, lawyers and management so that we could avoid a bankruptcy. Not only that, but we managed to bring the company out of this episode stronger than before. This was only possible due to strong, long-term relationships based on mutual trust. Two and a half years later, the company was successfully sold to British Telecom.

While business schools and universities may teach you valuable techniques for running a business, the networking topic is strangely absent from the curriculum. It is imperative to make a conscious decision to start networking as early as you can. Those contacts that you make at the start of your career will grow with you as you go along and often they will rise in their organizations to a higher level just as you may in yours. Thus, this early group will become your network's most solid foundation. You will know them well, as you will have known them for a long time, and they will be in places where you are even more valuable to each other than you are today.

Relationships are like an exquisite wine, the older the better.

Chapter 1

Networking the Old-Fashioned Way

The definition given earlier for networking is: *Building and maintaining relationships to establish a trust basis for the long term.*

As with any successful endeavor, one must always be actively engaged, pursuing a set of goals. Networking is no exception. No matter how you may choose to partake, expect investment of some time and money. Needless to say, make sure you enjoy doing it and that it provides an unlimited scope of activity!

Remember, networking demands that you invest a lot of time—including a lot of evenings and weekends. Working globally can even be a non-stop job in this day and age.

Integral to effective networking is patience. It must be done gently. Liaisons with decision makers can be a bit of a challenge as they are reserved and skeptical. Developing a sound foundation for what will become a mutually beneficial relationship with them takes time. This is time well spent.

Never consider networking simply facilitation to selling goods or services to your contacts. Use these events to arrange a happening or, even, work against something. Here you will have the opportunity to acquaint yourself with a unique crowd, eclectic in their interests, nationalities, languages, and customs. Often inspiring, usually of value, networking is also a lot of fun!

There are a number of different ways you can start building your network, such as events, seminars, peer-to-peer networking events, individual meetings or even chance meetings.

Where possible you need to prepare for these meetings, you also have to gain the interest of the people you are meeting with, find something in common. And you should not forget to start using the electronic tools you have available as early on as possible. Enter the name of your contact in your CRM so that you can annotate it with other information which you may need later on. Neither should you forget to follow up after such a meeting within twenty-four hours or so, whether by phone call or e-mail. And last, but certainly not least, in all cases continually think of what you have to offer your new contact instead of just the other way around. Your contact has to have an interest to want to work with you, to get to know you better.

One way of proactively building a network is by organizing well-targeted networking events. For instance, assemble small groups who have the same interests, that is, CIOs working in varied industries spanning verticals, perhaps young High Potentials who have the skill and are slated for senior or board positions in a few years. With these demanding groups you must ensure well-targeted content, otherwise, it will be only a one-off event in which will not provide an opportunity to strengthen or build on your network.

Draw your groups together with an acknowledged industry icon to speak on a topic close to their interests. Thus, you can build an atmosphere for exchange of experience and expertise. An event that is well matched to a targeted group is the key to success.

Commonality of topic breeds an environment which fosters the N Factor so fundamental to networking. The audience experience is enhanced by the speakers themselves, their expertise and topic forming the environment for aligned thinkers to network. Smaller events allow all the participants to get to know each other well. Don't forget to provide a contact list for all attendees of those who did attend and distribute to all upon their departure.

At these events, a fundamental idea that is on the forefront of your mind as well as those you are engaging in a dialogue with should be "How can I benefit from this event...and what can I offer?" This idea will endure beyond the events and can lead to the development of mutually beneficial dialogues.

The very first contact is often the most difficult. You can plan carefully to meet people; however, timing is often an important factor. Taking the initiative with smaller, better targeted events often pays off as you, the organizer, can structure an event such that you achieve your goals. The event-planning theme is noted throughout this book. As you organize events pay attention to catering to a homogeneous group with common interests. Those in attendance will experience successful networking opportunities. Repeating the event ensures maintenance of valuable contacts made at earlier gatherings as well.

A good example of the above is a forum such as the one we organized in Dallas in late 2006 together with the Southern Methodist University (SMU) for CXOs from Texas. The event was based on a subject that is current, the role of the CIO in a modern organization. While the content is very important, with speakers from key companies like ExxonMobil, PepsiCo and Chiquita Banana, it is also of importance to attendants that they meet, exchange information, experiences, and of course, business cards so that the initial contact can be continued at their convenience.

My experience has been that larger events, trade shows, and so forth, lack the intimacy of contact to allow the best networking unless you prepare well. Otherwise, these events will result more in a business card collection activity and quick chats instead of leading to a more meaningful and valuable communication. Often the nature of a tradeshow means that it is too quick and short to really talk to someone and get to know them, or even to meet with pre selected people that might be important to your network. For me, these events become frenetic and without the substance required to further develop a viable and productive network.

If you want to use these types of large events to extend your network, try and find a way of getting a list of participants upfront. From that list, select five to ten people you would really like to speak with; make sure to maintain a limited number. Use search engines on the Internet to find out as much as possible about your selected persons so that you are well prepared when you do get your chance to speak to them. Everyone is susceptible to someone who seems to be knowledgeable about their achievements and activities. Even in this area, technology can assist in creating a better foundation for your networking.

Recently, we spoke with Mitra van Raalten, an entrepreneur with a background in the travel industry. During her career, she experienced this same problem and has now developed a tool together with a number of business partners to solve exactly this issue – how to pre-select the people that are worthwhile talking to at these large events. The tool is called "Matchwork."

Matchwork© will enable people to get back in touch with other people based on the following principles:

- Development of value added content based on input by those people themselves; "by people for people"

- Mixture of elements of "strong" and "weak" ties

- Cross bordering of all kind of social levels of society and business settings

Set of examples:

Market	Matchwork© field of operation	Examples
Congresses (one day/multiple days) National and International	Connecting visitors and participants prior, during and after the event. Creation of value-added input for this community	Congress Centers, Foundation of Education, NGO's.
Network organizations	Co-development with organizations that are focused on networking.	OHM Inc., The European Centre of The Experience Economy, Club of Budapest
Event/Concerts	Visitors get access to Matchwork© when buying an entrance ticket	Concert brokers and ticket offices
Educational Institutions	Stimulation of community, own campus, connecting	Middle and Higher Education, Universities

(Online) Educational Institutions	With online offering of all kinds of education tools; possible to create a community (instead of only one to one) this is without borders of time and location	Digital University
Individuals	Connecting to create a marketplace for content	The-E-Factor *(www.the-e-factor.biz)*, *Hyves.nl*, *www.wineandfood-professionals.com*
Corporate Companies	Community, connecting, knowledge management, internal communication, HR, social mapping	McDonalds, chain companies (hotels, food organizations, etc.)

If you are focused on networking, even random contacts can turn into relevant contacts for your network. Flying 250,000 miles a year, you can imagine I meet many people during flights. Some of the contacts in my network today, stretch back to flights I took over twenty years ago.

These coincidental encounters require very rapid follow up. Doing so at least within twenty-four hours is wise. In your follow up, clearly refer to that which held your common interest (the film, book or other topic of interest) that provided fuel for the two of you to share ideas and interests.

This may sound a little obvious, but to best take advantage of these random encounters make sure you have something to say. Being able to answer the question "what do you do?" is essential. An exhaustive knowledge of your enterprise and the market segment in which it operates is a given. But go beyond this. Develop broad knowledge of general topics. Imagine how valuable the discussion will become when you speak knowledgably of the profession of your counterparty, or even share appreciation and interest in the arts, cooking, music, and the like. You don't have to be a renaissance man, but it doesn't hurt to have a general knowledge of your contact's interests.

Keeping current with matters of (global) politics, business, and world events is a valuable weapon. As these spheres impact your ventures, current knowledge of them is essential. The value of this knowledge can serve a similar purpose as that noted above. It is a worthy endeavor to read several papers and magazines. Comprehensive understanding of what is going on in politics, corporate, as well as public life, and in the markets—M&A activity, New Issues/IPOs—are all fodder for good conversation. Needless to say, if your skill indicated here has an international flavor, it adds depth and complexity to your presentation.

Whether at preplanned events or simply during the

course of living one's life, many of the contacts made have inherent and long-term value. Access to these contacts on demand is essential to best avail of the network. Fortunately, modern technology fosters enhanced cataloguing and retrieval through CRM software of which there are quite a few examples. The old Rolodex has had its day—the increasing time pressures of contemporary (global) business demand a system which gives you immediate and easy access to information or allows you to set alerts to key events.

Yes, technology is a core element to building and maintaining networks on such a large scale. However, the essential element of networking will always be the people. You must always invest the time to visit your contacts face-to-face when possible.

Another method of accelerating building your network is by tapping into the network of someone else. The trust basis between you and the person who introduces you to their network is of critical importance. Without that trust people will be very defensive of opening up their network and contacts to you. I have experienced this a number of times. For instance, I was recently appointed to a board and asked one of the other board members for an introduction to someone he knew. His (fairly blunt) answer was "I don't know you well enough yet." Again, this emphasizes the fact that you will first have to build a trust relationship before approaching someone to share networks.

Once you have achieved the basis on which the other will introduce you to their network, it goes without saying that this creates the obligation on you that you will treat the other's contacts with the utmost respect and carefulness.

Global Networking

The global economy introduces a "wild-card" into the process. A plethora of customs adds to the challenge of building and nurturing good, mutual dealings.

In the United States it is quite acceptable to call just about anything a networking event. In Europe you have to be much more careful with this term. Nevertheless, in the U.S., networking has become an art form, which can vary from a charity event to speed dating; it is commonly accepted to choose the most efficient format to getting to know as many people as possible in as little possible time. It is no surprise that the "elevator pitch" was born in the U.S.: tell who you are, what you do and everything else between the third and sixth floor! And this approach always results in superficial and casual interactions rather than in deep and durable relationships.

Networking is sometimes seen as a clubby event. For example, in the U.S., there are many so-called professional "clubs." In these clubs, everybody knows one another and, where possible, will help each other. Becoming a member of such a club can be very beneficial to your network, particularly in the U.S. This can be a country club, a university club or a club such as the prestigious Bohemian Club in San Francisco. It is not always easy to join one of these, as in almost all cases there will be great scrutiny, strict balloting and a long waiting list. However, it is an excellent way of meeting people who in turn are well connected. In these club environments, you will meet like-minded people: individuals with a common interest or a common background. Most of these clubs do have strict rules regarding business transactions – you can meet people at the club, but business is actually done outside its walls.

In the same manner as the example of clubs in the U.S., each country has its own specific formats and structures when it comes to networking. They might be political, dependent on the school you attended such as Oxford or based on companies that you may have worked for such as McKinsey's, IBM or Procter & Gamble. They may be located across different countries, different cultures and different languages but they share a common background.

In the global economy "Culture Gapping" is an absolute necessity as many business transactions will take place across various countries or even continents. Culture Gapping is the quick establishment of a sound relationship between two or more parties from different cultures, based on the common denominator that each implicitly trusts the party that introduced them to each other.

Of course, you need to understand the culture of the country that you want to do business with. Moreover, you will also need to build relationships or if possible, friendships with people in those countries to help you further. This is where the term "Think Global, Act Local" comes to mind.

Also bear in mind that there will be numerous soft rules depending on the culture. When you are visiting a country for a few days on a business trip, you will see the airport, various offices, taxis, and hotels. During these sorts trips it is often impossible to really start to understand the underlying elements of the culture you are visiting. When I started to travel to the U.S. in the mid eighties I often had the habit of wanting to set meetings on exactly the wrong days. For instance, one time I flew to the U.S. when the Super Bowl was on and everyone—literally everyone—was in front of the television. Or I announced that I was coming over "next Thursday" only to encounter a baffled silence followed by "but don't you know it's Thanksgiving?" This is not a good way to start your business relationships. It is worthwhile investing time to learn about the unspoken rules, holidays, and national interests of the country you want to do business with. This will show that you have an understanding and respect for that specific country.

In the Netherlands you are not going to be popular if you want to come over on April 30th (Queen's Day) or want to meet for dinner on the night the Dutch soccer team is playing against Germany. Or in the UK, on November 5th all families will be thinking about Guy Fawkes bonfires and there, children will be roaming the streets collecting a "penny for the Guy."

In France you have "Quatorze Juillet" – Bastille. On

"Quatorze Juillet" you will not find anyone in the office. The French spend time with their family and will find it disrespectful if you ask for a meeting on that day. If you are visiting these countries you should not only know to avoid these days for doing business, but you should also understand what these days mean to the nation.

Similarly, it is good to know that it is pointless wanting to make appointments in the month of August in France, Spain, and Italy. Everyone will be on holiday, visiting the seaside with their families. In the U.S., UK and even the Netherlands and Germany holidays are much more often spread so therefore you can continue to visit people in these areas over the summer period.

Another element that is of importance in this light is knowing the political systems of countries you work with. Most democratic countries have a dual party system, where you have left- and right-wing parties with one of these in parliament and the other as opposition. This often will have its influence on the business world. On the other hand, you have the Netherlands where consensus is very important (the so-called "polder model") and where you always have a political coalition in power.

At the end of this book you will find numerous examples of each country's approach to networks, provided by people from these regions.

Chapter 2

Maintaining Your Network

The creation of a network is hard enough. One's long-term credibility among contacts demands much consistent investment of time, effort, and patience.

However, maintenance of a network is often as challenging as creating one. Most of my contacts originated many years in the past, some even decades. The payoff is that these long-term contacts have generally moved up the ladder in their careers as I have. We are now at a much higher level in our respective organizations and industries than when we first met. The lesson I learned from these experiences was that you need to start building your network consciously as early as possible, and you need to structure it well in order to make sure you don't lose any of your contacts. Over time, your contacts will become more and more valuable – both from an interpersonal perspective as well as a business one.

There are many different ways to maintain contact. Obviously, you have all the electronic means of this day and age such as e-mail and VOIP, but electronic communications should only supplement face-to-face contact. In order to really continue building on your network you will have to make a reasonable effort to travel to wherever contacts happen to be.

When well nurtured and maintained, your networking contacts can lead to significant business opportunities. With regard to maintenance, you have to count on meeting your contacts at least once every six months or so, be it for lunch, a visit or a round of golf. Should you schedule an event, certainly invite them as guests.

Network maintenance requires sophisticated database organization, thus should be fully automated. It is advisable to divide your contacts into a few categories:

- Friendly, Long-term Relationships

- Good Business Relationships

- Casual Contact (you may have met at some point, and might be good to get to know better)

Friendly, Long-term Relationships

These are people with whom you have a long-standing friendly relationship. You will have to see them at least twice a year as indicated earlier. Needless to say, as these are friends, you will want to.

Include them in your social and business life whereby you bring people together who share a mutual interest, be it political, artistic, in business or sport. Keep these gatherings small, no more than four people sharing a meal or a round of golf.

The short "hello" is an additional element to be used here, either delivered by phone or e-mail. Perhaps you are to be visiting their country or simply want to express best wishes for a birthday or birth of a child.

I have often tried to share my love of art with my contacts by sending them a hand-chosen or specially designed item at Christmas. Not merely opting to choose for a Christmas card produced by the thousands, but the choice of something to reflect the special relationship I feel we have, is always much appreciated by the recipient.

Good Business Relationships

One's objective with these relationships demands maintenance such as meeting the contact face-to-face at least once a year. Here the venue can be a targeted event or simply, a concert or a round of golf. The planning element is key here. It is true that one's busy lives often distract us from the smooth coordination of all the people and places network maintenance requires. Nonetheless, an efficient CRM system, is imperative to allow you to establish categories which can be sub-divided through geography. Often you will find some spare time (curious how the "spare time" we find is often so little, isn't it?) while visiting certain countries and cities. When planning these trips, make sure to account for contacts in that location even if they are not your primary reason for the visit. Your network will appreciate being informed with a note saying something like "Hey, I'm in town on...are you free to meet up while I'm here?" Whether they can or can't, the network is maintained.

Keep them "in the loop" with regular e-mails about a new product introduction or an event that you are hosting. Use a single event as a reason to send out multiple e-mails. You can announce it with details of the program. Follow up later to inquire about their plans to attend. This will keep you on their radar for an extended period.

And of course, the ubiquitous Personal Digital Assistant (PDA) or cellular telephone allows you to choose any moment to let someone know you are thinking of them and the working relationship you both share.

Casual Contact

This group is one with whom you maintain contact through mass mailings, general announcements, newsletters and the like. It is always useful sending something to these people on a biannual basis.

It has repeatedly been shown that casual contacts are very useful, often necessary, when you seek a contact in a specific industry or geography. These contacts are very valuable when, for example, you are starting something from scratch. I began my expansion into New York and

San Francisco this way. If you know two or three people in the targeted industry or geography already, it is not very hard to leverage these contacts such that you can have ten to twenty contacts of a desired profile in a relatively brief time. In a sense, building a network of contacts is like building wealth: the first $100,000 are the hardest to gain!

As with each category of contacts, expect to spend a lot of time on their maintenance. A valuable lesson about contacts: categorize them immediately after establishing them for easy future reference.

It does seem a daunting task: maintaining your network at all times. Most do find it difficult – and, it does go without saying that you do have to enjoy people and the social whirl that the process demands.

Don't short change yourself by trying to use short cuts to build and maintain your network. I cannot emphasize enough that networking is not about going to an exhibition and collecting hundreds of random business cards.

Many people that I have met dislike those who are superficial and insincere in their interest. These "would-be-networkers" are always on the lookout for others whom they feel may be more important to them than the one with whom they are currently engaged in a conversation. These are "pseudo-networkers" who fail to see value in being informed about individuals and are not selective relative to the few people and small group who they really would like to meet for their mutual benefit.

The best relationships are ones that exist above the limitations imposed by strict segregation of personal and work contacts. When building and keeping a network, don't erect insurmountable barriers between personal and work relationships. People, not things, hold a good business together. For a business to operate more efficiently, a senior manager is advised to be much less concerned about managing transactions and pay more attention on managing relations. Transactional responsibility should more often be the province of subordinate staff.

When wisely used, the recent advances in technology wonderfully facilitate the art of networking. Keep in mind that it facilitates, but does not replaces your networking strategy. In fact, the increased use of technology means that personal contact based upon trust, mutuality and even reciprocity are almost even more important. And certainly, it is even more appreciated if you do maintain a personal contact consistently with your relationships.

Events

To enhance and extend your network, both relative to its scope and depth, organizing events is an ideal method. For many years we have arranged numerous events for exactly this reason. While organizing one, it is essential to set goals for yourself and have an understanding of how it will be experienced by those who attend.

Again you should expect to make a heavy investment of time and energy. This is relationship building! Quality guests result in you sponsoring a quality event. A personal invitation from you goes a long way in sponsoring a successful event. To completely delegate this responsibility is a big mistake. Be involved!

For example, in order to maintain and expand our network, one of my companies sponsored classical concerts inviting about 150 people at a time. I was strongly involved in the selection process of the guests and I would always do the seating myself – choosing who would sit with whom. Soon enough I realized that one way of making sure you do get to see everyone in person at the event was to stand at the door and personally welcome your guests.

The concerts were always a big hit, even to the extent that people were offended if they were *not* invited. On the one hand, this was obviously due to the quality and attractiveness of the event. On the other, it very clearly achieved *status* factor among peers (as in "Oh, I was invited to this-

and-this. Weren't you?").

When the company for which we organized these concerts changed ownership, they continued to sponsor them. However, instead of the personal approach we had taken, people were now invited "professionally" with luxuriously printed mailings. The result was more and more empty seats. Instead of attracting the well-targeted audience we had aimed at before, it became an event with no coherence relative to the type of people attending. Needless to say, the audience dwindled. My intent is not to boast about our networking prowess, but suggest this circumstance as an example of how you can influence the result and outcome of your event by your personal input and effort.

Other Events

The following are some other examples of events you can organize for networking purposes:

Sports Events

Tennis Clinics

We organized about ten of these in Europe and the U.S. Much of the attraction results from a famous player being the guest of honor. The format is always the same; a maximum number of participants (fifteen) and two well-known players, such as Nastase, Peter Fleming or Okker. The event begins with a one-hour lesson. And then of course it is very exciting for guests to engage in one-on-one, or many-to-one net-play with the visiting celebrity pros. Our pleasing day of tennis was nicely rounded off with dinner. Often tall or at least exaggerated stories of the day's play were entertaining topics of table conversation.

This particular event attracts two types of individuals. The first are the tennis fanatics. They simply thrive on the opportunity to engage in net-play with noted pros. The second come a single time to satisfy their curiosity. The latter group poses a great challenge. As the event organizer you seek guests who attend on multiple occasions and represent organizations at a senior, decision-making level. You can expect the tennis fanatics will be attending on a repeated basis although after three or four times the value of inviting them decreases rapidly. The latter group will probably come only once. Therefore, you will need to keep finding new participants that fit your target of an appropriate guest.

This type of networking event has a limited lifespan. Although you as the organizer will reap great benefit in your relationships with those who attend, and they will remember it for a long time, you have to realize that once you have repeated the event a few times with the same people – it will loose its attraction. You can prolong the success by bringing the formula to another geography as I did, moving it from Europe to the U.S. for a different group of relationships. This means at least you can reap the benefit of the organization of such an event. The first one will require the most effort and time; repetition is often much simpler.

Soccer

In Europe, soccer is one of the most popular sports in terms of number of people watching and in terms of interest. In the past fifteen to twenty years, the business influence has grown dramatically. This is largely due to sponsoring, VIP areas, and hospitality packages. This influence has obviously been greatly fed by television and other media – a top game can mean that millions are watching it.

There are a variety of ways you can use soccer games to stimulate your networking activity. For instance, I have been a long-term member of Ajax* with a season ticket for the past ten years. This means that I have been able to add contacts to my network even here. You are ensured of a common interest already and you will meet people on a regular

* Soccer club from Amsterdam, The Netherlands

basis to slowly get to know them better. These sports clubs often even have a business club attached, of which you can become a member.

Then as a company, you can sponsor soccer in a variety of ways. In some cases we were the sub-sponsor for the Dutch soccer club (FC Utrecht†) or in some cases even the main sponsors, such as for our local soccer club (NAC‡) with the name and logo of the company displayed on the player's jerseys. The main reason we choose to do this is for branding and name-recognition. And of course, because you realize in advance that there are significant amounts of people watching the games.

Soccer clubs often go out of their way to provide sponsors with facilities such as special VIP rooms and hospitality suites which can be used for networking activities. However, although this is useful as a marketing activity, from a pure networking viewpoint it is quite difficult to achieve a cost versus gain balance.

Of the seventeen regular competition games, only about five are that attractive that you will easily persuade people to attend. In Europe, soccer matches are often played on weekends. Add to that the fact that soccer is still seen to be a man's sport, and quite simply few women are interested in soccer. So as your contact may be busy all week in their business role you would be vying with the spouse for their relatively limited free time on the weekends.

Then there is the fact that each game takes up a rela-

† Dutch soccer club.
‡ NAC is a Dutch soccer club from Breda.

tively long time and given the noise from the public during the game, there is not really a chance to have a meaningful conversation. In short, it is often too difficult to get the right people to the game. The exception of course is the two or three top games a year for which you do not even have to ask people to come; you will be getting so many requests for tickets that you could not possibly honor them all without going bankrupt.

In short, although soccer does offer some opportunities to apply the N Factor, this may be more in the arena of meeting new people through a membership or achieving name recognition through sponsorship. The actual events you can organize will undoubtedly be enthusiastically achieved by some of your soccer-fan contacts, but will not deliver as much in terms of deepening the relationship, or good business conversation as some other events we describe in this book.

Golf

Golf is a hobby that fits well within an executive's arsenal of diversion and it allows for advancement of a corporate agenda and related networking. Relative to the imperative of communication and association for business purpose, it is well accepted and effective to maintain current relationships and court new ones. But never forget to first think about the course itself, one that challenges the participants and provides the amenities that make for an experience that is both pleasant as an athletic endeavor as well as fertile for the networking ambitions to manifest themselves. One such locale is Echolake in New Jersey whose infrastructure and course meet the above criteria. On repeated occasions, this venue has more than satisfactorily met my networking objectives. This location through one event, has allowed us to further the interests of a charity, the city of Amsterdam, our corporate networking partners and ourselves. I will explain more about this in the later section titled "Networking and Charities."

Pay particular attention to organizing this type of event well. As there can be many people participating, often about 100, you must be meticulous in devising the schemes in which your guests are coordinated in their play. Groups that play well together, network well together too. This will reflect positively on you as the event organizer. You have created an environment of good strokes, both in terms of golf and of those relating to initiation and/or development of mutually viable, leading to often beneficial and enterprising dialogues.

One of the nicest events that I have had a pleasure to attend was a Charity Golf event in Pittsburgh, USA organized by Andy Russell, a football icon in the Pittsburgh area and two time football winner in the mid seventies. He used his own network and contacts to organize this event and would invite his former teammates from his era to participate. Naturally, a large number of business people were keen to attend the event and in the process donate to the charity of Russell's choice which would literally raise

$100,000 for a children's charity each year. In fact, it was so popular that there would even be a waiting list.

The event had a number of elements that made it so attractive. First of all, this was a great chance for the Football players to be reunited with their former teammates. Second of all, they acted as a magnet for the business people for whom these players had been their youth-idols. A chance to meet with the players and even play and converse with them offered a great attraction. Consequently, this gathering stimulated networking amongst the business people participating in the event. For me, this is a perfect example of bringing different worlds together – sports, celebrities, business and charity.

Chess

This is networking modality that is aimed at a highly targeted audience. I was able to engage the then world champion Garry Kasparov and three other grand masters for a simultaneous chess-game. The small group of invitees highly appreciated this unique experience. Unfortunately, it did not lead to greatly facilitated networking dialogues, although it did add to the company's image in the eyes of those who were invited. The lesson in this case is to make sure that the event planned stimulates the minds of those who are invited. Make sure to provide a fertile environment that allows for a dialogue leading to further communication and a mutual possible engagement.

Automobile Racing

This is an activity in which we hope to have driven well. We created a car racing team, made up of three drivers. The one we had in the early nineties was extremely successful. They won several national championships, including the twenty-four-hour Francorchamps* in their grouping. This was a professional team that regularly appeared on European televised sports channels and, as such, was perceived very well. It even got to the point that a toy manufacturer launched a series of toy cars with the logo we had at that time, on it. Our corporate image, for my venture then, Rijnhaave, achieved great exposure and enhancement.

The hospitality in the racing circuit's facilities provided a strong sense of community among those invited. This allowed and spurred excellent networking experiences for our guests. Keep in mind, however, that the auto racing event does not have universal appeal due to its arousal of environmental concerns.

Cultural Activities

Concerts

For a period of ten years we have had the privilege of organizing semi-annual concerts of such renowned artists as the Pianist Evgeny Kissin, Cecilia Bartoli and cellist Yo-Yo Ma. Experience has shown that events of this type are very well suited to developing and strengthening existing relationships significantly. Contacts bring their spouses and enjoy the opportunity to experience world-class musical perform-

* Francorchamps is a famous Formula One circuit located in Belgium.

ances, after which comes an opportunity to socialize with the artists. It is an intimate setting. With these events, as with the others, you must ensure that you keep your own goals in terms of your target audience in mind, and make sure you conduct invitations in a personal manner. Without paying attention to these simple facts, the expected N Factor value to your business from this event will otherwise diminish over time.

I have very fond memories of such an event we organized where the musical artist we celebrated was the great American performer Ray Charles. Although not our standard event, the scope of his talent and unique nature of his artistic expression was welcomed by our audience and helped establish a fertile environment advancing the interests of those in attendance.

We conducted this in conjunction with the sale of Rijnhaave to British Telecom and organized it as a special evening for our contacts as a thank you. It was a small—about 175 people in all—but a truly fabulous and memorable concert that was talked about for many years.

To be able to have Ray Charles in such close vicinity that you could have touched him was very special indeed. Even for Ray. For a long time, he had not played in a trio. He told me later that he had almost felt nervous and had had to rehearse prior to this performance.

Fine Art

Similar to concerts there are other types of sponsoring

such as art exhibitions. Karel Appel is a titan in Dutch modern art represented in collections at major museums worldwide. Jan Sierhuis is another high profile Dutch artist. Painters such as these prove a great draw, attracting a lively, culturally aware, and influential group.

Others

Can the best way to a contact's heart be through their stomach? One of the most successful ways of networking we have yet found is to set up an evening cooking workshop for your contacts. Under the tutelage of a master chef, fifteen to twenty participants prepare their own gourmet meal. This event offers all the right ingredients for a memorable evening: generous quantities of laughter, lots of conversation, a dash of wine or juice – all stewing during the course of four hours whilst the guests prepare their dinner. The highlight obviously being the eating of the dinner they have prepared with their own hands.

Exercise scrutiny with those you invite– make sure you have the right mix at your event. One example of a good combination is when my company had Juan Soto do a presentation called "The Miracle of the Spanish Economy." This turned out to be a success because Mr. Soto is an eminent and well-respected businessman from Spain with contacts through European business and government at the highest levels. He is also a wonderful person to know with a great sense of humor and a superb knowledge of European history.

Having a renowned speaker each time assures repeat attendance and as members of the group return on a regular basis, it is definitely worth the effort. For example, at one of our current company's events we had the former Prime Minister of the Netherlands, Wim Kok, speak about the impact of outsourcing/offshoring on the Dutch economy. In this example, as Wim Kok is such a well-respected politician with a high degree of integrity, his presence was one of the key reasons people attended our event. As such, having well-known people or famous sportsmen participate or speak, adds extra dimension and attraction to your event.

In our experience, we find the best way of creating the best possible mix for an event is by adding an element of "fun" as in the above example of a group dinner party. Another example is our own High Potential group where after the keynote presentations we provide, for instance, a workshop in mixing cocktails or in DJ'ing. In all cases you must select a social diversion that matches the character of the group and creates a bond between the members. Participants will realize that they also need to network to advance their careers and their employer's agendas. When you have brought the group together successfully, they will enjoy future opportunities and will regularly get together.

One thing that we have done adds an extra dimension to that described above. The participants of our networking events are invited to join a password protected, "closed user group" on our website. This allows them to continue a liaison facilitated by us. This electronic forum, where they share information, chat or discuss business topics, adds value by perpetuating the good relations established between them during the event. By maintaining access to a similar "closed user group" on your website you will derive benefits as you become the dialogue facilitator among a wide scope of contacts.

Something a lot of people do not realize, but that we see often is that the people at the top of large organizations tend to have a very limited network. Frequently, their focus is internal. On many occasions their external contacts are almost exclusively based on the function and position of the organization. It is not rare that when these people retire or become unnecessary, they realize they are forgotten quickly and are no longer invited to events.

When organizing events, never lose sight of your goal. You have to try to be unique and the quality of an event's agenda is paramount. Quality does not always have to be expensive. However, you have to realize that your target audience will be regularly invited to similar events and will therefore have to consider the special character of the event and ultimately decide whether to attend yours or the event of someone else. Remember that these elements, together with your passion for your event and your audience, can take you far.

Is a Network Transferable?

Networking—in its micro sense—is communication between two people. In this case, its transferability is difficult to assess.

We will try to formulate an answer on the much-asked question "Is a network transferable?" based on the three different groups of contacts that you may have.

As mentioned earlier in this chapter, there are three types of possible contacts:

- Friendly, Long-term Relationships
- Good Business Relationships
- Casual Contact

Friendly, Long-term Relationships

These are very personal and based on trust, chemistry, and respect. Often, given the amount of history to them, these are very hard to transfer to another party. This is the type of contact where you often understand each other almost tacitly. Those relating in this manner are often of the same generation. Sometimes the closeness of this relationship can become a barrier of sorts. You or your counterpart may not be prepared to risk the relationship in order to sell something or to achieve a short-term gain. You may also be unnecessarily fraught with insecurity that you could make a mistake which might damage the relationship.

A wise approach in these situations is for the parties to bring in others who again have similar interests and are of a same generation; they may connect as well with each other as you do with your contact. Here you have created a new level of interaction, integrating an expanded dialogue between additional contacts. Those newly brought into this dialogue can extend the relationship between your organization and that of your contact.

Good Business Relationships

It is often easier to have someone else maintain the contact that you may have developed where there is a clear business basis and purpose for the relationship between you and a particular contact. You and your contact may still have personal preferences, but as long as you select the right person, transferability here is often not an issue. The introduction of a third party should mostly be seen as a backup or addition rather than a complete replacement though.

One word of caution: don't involve too many individuals. If you do, you will never create any depth to the relationship, and the other party (or parties) may feel they are of little or no importance to you.

Casual Contact

Here it is relatively easy to bring someone else in the picture. There is no joint history that you have built up as yet. There may even be a clear objective to introduce some-one else. We all get e-mails regularly from people we have met in past years that find themselves having to be in Amsterdam for business and think "Hey, I know someone there!" In this case it is quite easy to pass them on to some-one else located at the capital of the Netherlands, as there is a clear objective—find company, advice about the city or which hotel to choose, an introduction to another compa-ny—that is not tied to the initial person they may have met. Of course, this is also subject to your own judgment of how interesting this contact can be for you. If you think they could be of value, it is always worth investing the time and effort of answering their questions and spending some time with them during their stay.

In all cases mentioned above, it is very important to ensure that the person you would like to introduce as an additional party, backup or replacement fits with your con-tact in terms of interests, business or view on life in general.

The N Factor and Charities

Partnering with a charitable organization can be an excellent way of expanding your network. In the U.S. this is widely undertaken. It is increasingly more observed in European practice as well.

A common denominator among charities themselves is sophisticated marketing and networking. Access their websites and this is evident. It is an excellent example of the N Factor changing the dynamics and adding an extra dimension that neither party would achieve on its own. A charity seeks to be easily identified and there is a distinct relationship between their recognition and the ability to raise money. Usually those who are affiliated with given foundations, as board members or donors, belong to an eclectic and upscale group. The people that support the charity, will also share the concerns of the foundation, the rule of ensuring a common interest, is therefore clearly adhered to.

Earlier I made a reference to golf as an ideal event to further a multitude of networking interests. We devised one such event on behalf of "Little Hope," a charity supporting victims of the 9/11 tragedy. It was structured to achieve multiple ends. Twenty Tri-State (NY, NJ, and CT) companies were asked to complete a survey regarding their plans to expand their businesses to Europe within the next twelve to eighteen months. For each completed survey, our company, OHM Inc., made a contribution to "Little Hope." Those companies that completed the survey were invited to join in a golf outing coordinated by the city of Amsterdam.

Not only was money raised for "Little Hope," but we also provided the city of Amsterdam a forum to promote itself as an attractive location in which to realize European expansion. In fact, almost half in attendance made arrangements with Amsterdam to take the next step and explore its viability as a host of the companies' European presence. It allowed us introduction to and relationship with valuable contacts, both for ourselves and clients. Our activities provided us access to the wide scope of contacts of the city. In return for this valuable data, we paid the city commensurate with those completing the survey. This met our interests, those of Amsterdam, a deserving charity and whetted the appetites of those with European expansion in mind; a very clear example of adding an extra dimension for all parties concerned. And good golf too!

At present, I am working to avail of my network to create and support a mentor organization for the underprivileged. I am seeking not only to connect those more in need with mentors in large corporations, but I'm also seeking greater opportunities for these young people; allowing them to make a greater contribution to society and bettering their own lives. Here I am very pleased to have used my network for social benevolence as well as to realize its further growth.

Chapter 3
E-Networking Tools

Skilled use of networking tools is of great importance. My background is such that this should come as no surprise.

Consider the following:

1. Technology and communications have been common denominators throughout my career.

2. One's network—particularly in the global arena — can only be maintained using one or more networking tools described here.

If you base the maintenance of your network on simple telecommunications, you'll probably find that it will only be of limited size, thus limited benefit. Periodic face-to-face contact is necessary to enhance the dialogue and the relationship.

It took several years before I began to fully take advantage of the multitude of technologies available. At first, my assistant linked me to my network. Thus, it was her choice, not mine, as to how, with whom, and with what fervor I maintained the network.

Needless to say, this was an overly passive way to maintain and nurture such valuable contacts. Now, I and my partners are much more directly and proactively involved in maintenance and development of our networks. Modern electronics tools allow us to do this.

Ronald Plompe, formerly Director of KPN Royal Dutch Telecom ventures—the venture of the Dutch telephone company—and I have attempted to prepare an inventory of tools available that you can use to advance your networking interests.

We have endeavored to make this list both comprehensive, relative to options available to further one's network and user-friendly, particularly for those for whom IT is not their core business.

E-Networking Tools

When considering networking tools, there are many currently used that will assist you in achieving your goals.

E-mail

E-mail allows well-facilitated and inexpensive contact with your existing relationships as frequently as you choose.

It is also exceptionally well suited for immediate follow

up, as when you have first made contact and seek a sound foundation to the relationship. After meeting someone, it is very advisable to try and send an e-mail soon, thus ensuring that the other party remembers you. Keep this new dialogue warm, alive, and current; perhaps mutually beneficial. E-mail is becoming an integral part of Client Relationship Management (CRM) tools. This is enhanced by the CRM technology's ability to facilitate means of contact for a multitude of people from one easily accessed, organized and central place.

Although it does not replace long and formal letters, it enables communication of short and compact messages that are answered in a similar fashion by the other party. This is a new and different mode of professional communication, often with its own style and even language. Beware of the negative side of e-mail – by being inherently short and direct, the chance for miscommunication is greater if words are not chosen carefully.

It is interesting to see for instance, the creation of new terms such as "flame mail". As people are further removed from their counterparty in the electronic communication age (after all, you type on a keyboard, you do not speak with the person face to face), and the language is direct – it is also easier to use language that would never have been used in a professional letter. This can create, or is sometimes even intended as such, a correspondence which leaves nothing to the imagination but which is still totally inappropriate to professional conduct.

Tools such as the MailSpaces software by Kinomi, extends the capabilities of e-mail even further. It allows one or more people to communicate with others in a highly efficient manner. A registry of common themes in e-mails is developed through tracking those between aligned interest groups. This can be accessed at any given time by any member of the group, thus, creating a central database that can be researched easily and efficiently.

Customer Relation Management (CRM)

Current **CRM** systems have the advantage of offering a highly efficient method to organize many contacts. It allows you to make a selection based on function, role, location or industry. If you want to gather all your contacts in the financial services industry, you can easily create a list of those in this category. Equally, you can create selections for specific events (see Chapter 2). For example, you can classify contacts based on interests in sports, art or cooking. This will allow you to maintain contact based upon meeting the interests of a given individual and presenting to them an event with their interest parameters. Perhaps you have read an article that would interest them or experienced something else of mutual interest. This system will prompt you to keep your contacts "in the loop" as you define it. Without the likes of ACT, Goldmine, Salesforce et al, I don't know what I would do to keep my 5000+ contacts straight and easily accessed.

The delivery method of these systems had been very

critical in this development. Today, as a single user or small group, access to highly professional tools at a low cost is available through the ASP model that many now follow.

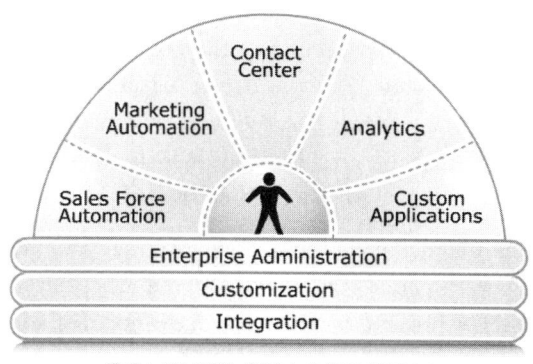

Complete CRM Solution *

Search Engines

Search engines, in themselves are not necessarily a networking tool. However, they can play a role in obtaining background information and doing research on people you seek to meet or have recently met. We have all become very accustomed to a variety of search engines with Google currently the best known. Other examples are Yahoo!, Microsoft, Lycos, and Gopher.

Sites such as Google, Yahoo! and others can facilitate the maintenance and creation of new network links,

* Image from http://www.salesforce.com/products/

through preparation for meeting a contact, perhaps for the first time. For instance, if you are preparing to go to a large scale event and you want to prepare to meet the four or five contacts that are of key interest, researching their names beforehand allows you to dive into the background of given people in a very easy, direct, and often comprehensive manner. This will allow you to better understand your chosen counterpart. Therefore, the seeds for a mutually enjoyable and useful dialogue are laid, given that which you have learned with regard to shared interests and priorities.

The interaction is further enhanced as your research shows you care, that you are interested in who they are and what they represent. When you have not met someone before, yet would like to, imagine the impact on meeting them when equipped with knowledge of who they are, what they do, and what matters to them. Keep in mind that information found on the Internet is not always objective. For instance, frequency of Internet presence and occurrence can be bought for a fee, thus distorting the reality to a degree.

Googling is also ideal to allow you to keep track of a contact's (or potential contact's) activities. As it is impossible to meet everyone in your network in person on a very regular basis, you usually want them to be aware that you are thinking of them. Searches can give you data on your contact, such as a new job, an article they may have written, an event they are speaking at, etc. Equipped with this knowledge, you are prepared to write or phone them to wish them well, congratulate them or make other comments.

Social Networking Software

Social networking on the Internet can manifest in different ways. Among these are blogs, interest forums and online chat groups. Each of these have a place in the context of furthering and maintaining your business network but are more powerful as purely social tools to establish contact with ex-colleagues or friends. Examples are given below in the "Many-to-many communication" section. The other element is the use of social networking tools such as LinkedIn, Plaxo, OpenBC, Orkut, SecondLife, and others.

According to Forrester Research, the percentage of American online consumers using social networking sites more than once a week, grew from 1 percent to 4 percent in 2005.* The same site reflects in October 2006 that "Social network sites are used by 17 percent of the European online population."

Ed Callahan Jr. of Momentum Technology Partners is a Career Technology Executive. Ed has been using LinkedIn for close to four years now, he considers LinkedIn to be particularly useful when engaged in segments on the fringes of his own industry experience. Ed identifies mainly human capital or human resources executives in target companies. He says, "By using the 'Find People' tab, I entered 'talent' in the key word section of the search terms. We believe that if there was a mid-to high-level HR manager with the term 'talent' in his/her title, then

---

* Report purchased from www.forrester.com on August 19, 2006.

that was a good litmus test which said this company was likely progressive and would most likely be open to new solutions to improve the quality of the employee hired. I then entered the name of the target company in the company field and 'VP' or 'Director' in the title field. LinkedIn returned a list of people in my network, who are, or have ever been, at the target company with a VP or director title and which contained the keyword 'Talent.' You can also limit the search to 'current' title and 'current' company by simply checking the appropriate boxes."

Ed continues, "There are a lot of other ways to use LinkedIn. For instance my favorite is help with time and territory management. LinkedIn made the prospecting and business development process much more effective for me than it has ever been in the past."

Another example that uses Social networking as the basis of their commercial activities is Zubka. Different from other social networks, Zubka looks to tap into its members' existing networks rather than asking members to create one through the site. Zubka therefore manages to flip the idea of online social networking on its head by creating real value in the virtual world for networks that exist in the physical world.

Echoes of eBay's model start to appear when you look at Zubka, which is ultimately a community of people trading information (instead of goods) where the platform takes a small cut. eBay and Zubka are examples of sites that use the networks people can reach (eBay) as well as have (Zubka) as the basis for a business opportunity.

It is interesting to look at the way younger generations are using tools to network. The connections this group makes are currently largely happening via weblogs, wiki's, podcasts, social bookmarking sites and in closed communities. A good example of the latter is Hyves. This online network was founded by Raymond Spanjaar, Floris Rost van Tonningen and Koen Kam in Amsterdam, the Netherlands in October 2004.

In his book, *Hyve Society,* Bee Wilson's proposition is that humans have always viewed the beehives as a miniature universe with order and purpose and looked to the hive to make sense of human society.*

Hyves is largely based on these principles which are for instance also the same principles as the slightly older American online network, *Orkut.com.* The start of Hyves was initially focused on the friends of the founders, and their surrounding student networks. It then started spreading to other student cities in the Netherlands and beyond. Now Hyves is also attracting younger age groups as well as those in their thirties. A friend will send an invite to join Hyves to a contact via e-mail. Once registered the new member gets their own page through which they can control and maintain their network (friends, friends of friends), profile, photos and e-mails. Other Hyvers can leave a "doodle" (quick comment) on that page and friends can write an

* (Economist 23rd September 2005).

endorsement.

With the option "Who, What, Where (www)" the Hyvers can note on the site what they are doing at any given time. And you can log-in via **SMS** to the site, with a location notification for **MSN** Messenger. For instance, "Brenda is sunning in Vondel Park."

A member of Hyves can register for one of the many sub-Hyves—which can be either public or purely private— where one can exchange messages about a certain topic. This goes all the way from "Happy Single Hyves" to the more obscure "Hyves for the Nose Ape" or general interest Hyves such as student societies, sports or cities (for instance: Amsterdam City.)*

Since October 2004, *Hyves.nl* has grown to a total number of Hyvers of 2.6 million and continues to grow further by thousands of users each day. Although originally founded in the Netherlands, 1 million users are currently in South America and the site is available in seven languages. Hyves is unusual in that it gets used for a very wide variety of purposes – from online chatting to video/photo sharing, doodling and many other methods used to communicate with fellow students, interest groups, family or friends and colleagues. In the Netherlands, the Prime Minister Mr. Jan Peter Balkenende (with over 30,000 connections) and the Leader of the Opposition, Mr. Wouter Bos (20,000 friends) have both become "Hyvers".

For a long time, Hyves shied away from having any type

* Volkskrant, March 2005

of advertising on the site. However, since September 2005, advertising is permitted as long as it follows the Ten Commandments set by the management and voted on by Hyvers themselves:

Ten Commandments for Hyvertisements*

1. Thou shalt offer something to Hyvers

2. Hyvers shall receive discount

3. The Hyver shall have the final say. (Under each advertisement, Hyvers can vote)

4. A maximum of one ad per page is allowed

5. The majority of the page shall remain free of advertising

6. Offerers of samples, premiere tickets or other gifts will receive extra views in a specially targeted format.

7. Thou shalt not provide falsified testimonials to a Hyver

8. Thou shalt not provide pop-ups, lay-overs, pop-unders or any other blood pressure raising type of expressions.

9. Thou shalt meet and treat others as one wishes oneself to be met and treated.

10. Thou shalt refrain from using wildly babbling,

---

* Ten Commandments were published in a press release issued by the founders on September 26, 2005 and posted in the following link:
http://www.hyves.nl/index.php?l1=ut&l2=ab&l3=ns&pressmessage_id=23.
Ten Commandments translated by Marion Freijsen.

psychotically expressing, erotically dancing hippos and other mentally retarded animals.

Hyves is already being used as a one-on-one communication tool by universities for educational purposes instead of the standard electronic learning environment. Furthermore it is also interesting for one-to-many communication such as for instance by Jimmy Woo, the famous Dutch nightclub, who uses it to communicate with its clients and send out invitations to special parties. Or H&M, the fashion chain, which has created a following of 34,000 Hyvers in a separate "Hyve." Hyves manages to achieve a very high interactivity frequency between its members.

One of the reasons we have chosen to highlight Hyves, is that it serves as a prime example of the fact that this type of site is proving to be a very popular method of networking for the younger generations (fifteen to thirty years old). It is based on the combination of both having similar interests, personally knowing one another and the use of technological tools that are available to the group. Because of its simplicity and low barrier to entry, Hyves has attracted a large number of people in a very short space of time, while the founders ensured that it did not turn into a purely commercial site whereby e-mercials create a high level of frustration among users but where advertising is embedded in the structure and purpose of the closed community. I think we are only at the beginning of this type of networking and I am convinced that this way of networking will slowly gain ground in the business world largely because of the international aspects. The likes of *Hyves.nl* can offer an interesting combination of traditional networking (largely dependent on personal contact) and new technologies and is therefore one to watch.

Social networking brings people together in many ways. A system such as LinkedIn can provide an additional manner of support to your networking activities. Nevertheless, these tools will never replace the traditional networking methods such as the ones described in various other sections in this book. One of the reasons is that networking must have the element of offering something to both parties and personal contact. These systems can technically accommodate this, although the people you will find using the system are very much on the demand side only. Networking then becomes much more of a one-way street and you have to ask yourself whether people you do not know will react to your request or invitation. If they do react, there will be a natural element of caution to their response. It is also very difficult to ascertain whether someone is a "warm" contact of one of the other people in your network or whether they have merely clicked "yes" when invited to join the network used. This comes back to the question of "Is a network transferable?" which was described earlier.

You must ask yourself whether the people who are at a sufficiently high level in those organizations that you would like to add to your network, are sincerely joining such systems or just responding to invitations. I am familiar with a number of people at board level who do not even have an e-mail address. They wish to protect themselves from unsolicited queries. It seems that the people on the demand side of the equation are the ones availing of such networking tools. They often want something and seek contact. Those whose contact they seek don't necessarily want them to have it.

In an effort to achieve heightened awareness, we undertook a survey called "Networking Software" among our own contacts in one of these systems. The results show a very interesting pattern.

We sent out this survey* to a large number of our contacts, yet received response from less than 14 percent. In itself this is an interesting fact. All of those to whom we sent the survey asked us to join them in this social networking tool. Given the very low response rate, it would appear that people are more interested in using the system than to be used by it. This observation is strengthened as, although some people have a network of many thousands of contacts in the system, the majority of the replies state that they mostly use it professionally to find new contacts or employees.

The survey shows that each user, on average, only got 3.1 lasting business contacts out of using the system. This underscores the fact that although you can show a great network, it does not actually deliver much that you did not have before. Is this system one that appeals mostly to those who

---

* Survey sent to 154 contacts on January 25, 2005.

want to get something from others?

The conclusion we reach here is relevant if looking at the current generation at the top of organizations worldwide. However, the new generation—High Potentials and Starting Entrepreneurs—who is entering its names and titles today, will most likely continue to update profiles as it climbs the corporate ladders and advances in its careers. Therefore, these systems will increase in value over time and become a more acceptable tool to use both within and to extend your network. It is also highly likely that such systems will develop their own (unspoken) rules of conduct as time progresses.

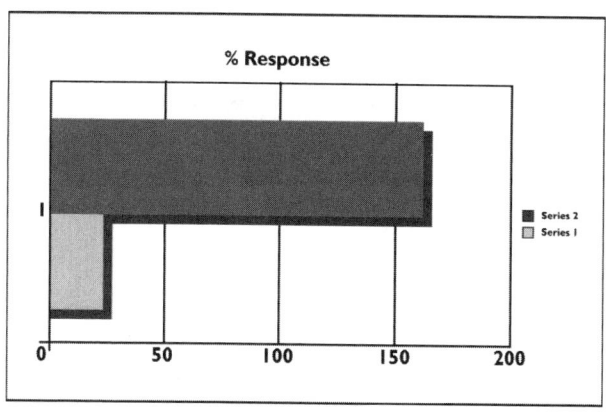

Picture IV.1. Responses from survey

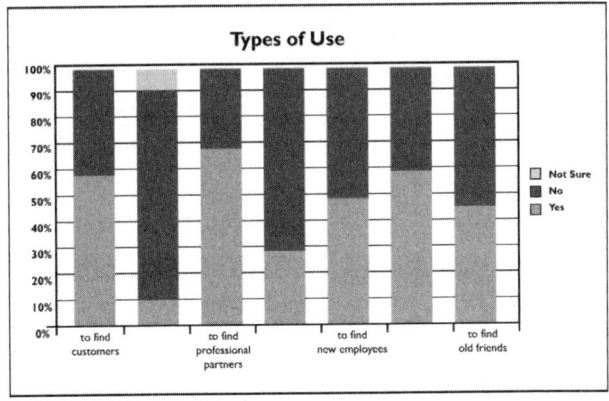

Picture IV.2. Types of use of networking software

Collaboration Tools

Every day, millions log on to instant messaging systems to share ideas, find answers and make connections. The power of collaborative knowledge has profoundly changed how we all do business.

Collaboration software allows concurrent users to share resources, communicate, and work on a single project from separate workstations. It also provides integrated services and Internet-based collaborative software development to enable business management solutions, business and community transformation, and innovation. It does all this while delivering substantial return on investment. Common examples are IBM Lotus Sametime, Lotus Notes, Microsoft Live

Communication Server and Office Communicator.

Collaboration tools are extremely useful in a work environment. Their application to furthering professional networking is also profound.

That which is applicable to organizations is also applicable to individuals in the networking arena. Collaboration tools allow you to maintain contact with groups of people. However, they must be strategically used. Consider the following:

1. Since most collaboration tools are discrete from the process, users must first find the appropriate tool to fit the circumstances.

2. Users are then directed to the appropriate collaboration tool (for example, instant messaging, web conferencing or, team-ware) from a palette of services or via application linking.

3. Even if you use your collaboration software from within another application (such as your work portal), you will still need to do your preparation work to collaborate effectively (for example, set up the space, invite people, and post documents).

Once you have determined the different communication types, a further division can be made in the communication forms one-to-one, one-to-many, many-to-one, and many-to-many. Examples of all of these are given in figure

IV.4.

One-to-One Communication

In networking, one-to-one communication is the most traditional form. This includes, of course, face-to-face meetings and dialogues as well as Internet usage. Despite the greater informality attached to electronic communication relative to traditional meetings, it is essential to maintain common courtesy as best you can.

One-to-Many Communication

This includes such things as mailshots, briefings, and newsletters.

When engaging in one-to-many communication, all the rules for regular mail should apply. After all, communication with a large group of one mail message or post is more or less the same as communicating with one person. However, the possibility of offending a great many more people with one ill-advised remark demands great scrutiny. You simply must gear your message very carefully to your audience.

Many-to-One Communication

In a network environment, you will be unlikely to use this type of communication. Such an example is where many publishers may target one author for the copyrights of a book.

Many-to-Many Communication

In the case of many-to-many, one could think of group discussions where teamwork is employed to satisfy the objective of a common task. For networking purposes, this could be a common interest groups or the use of blogs or chat groups. It is important to focus on the goals you wish to achieve when using these tools. As an example of application of a tool in this case, the blog allows you to maintain a live and continuous dialogue where those of similar perspectives can meet and share ideas.

There are different types of chat sessions. Chat rooms with a particular industry focus serve a similar purpose as do blogs in meeting new people. Setting up a closed password protected user group on your website, as we have done at OHM, facilitates communication among groups you have brought together; groups that exist through your efforts and can be nurtured through your creation of a closed user group.

Chat is something currently used mostly between people who know each other well already (colleagues, friends and such), but you should expect the use to increase and spread among a wider audience over the next years and it is likely to form an essential component of networking in future. Examples are Skype, Microsoft's MSN or Yahoo!'s IM.

The various types are depicted below:

	Uni directional	Bi directional
One 2 One		
One 2 Many		
Many 2 One		
Many 2 Many		

Figure IV.3. Different communication forms *

By combining the above types of communication forms with the different types of commonly used descriptions such as real-time/non-real-time, you can form the following groupings of tools:

* Picture IV.3. Provide by Ronald Plompen, Flyzone B.V.

| | Real Time | | Non Real Time |
	Asynchronus	Synchronus	Asynchronus
Uni Directional	threading, e-rooms	conversation, chat	leaflets, e-mail, videomail, voicemail, fax, paging
	e-rooms, streaming audio, video	audio, web conferencing, application sharing, moderated chat	television, videotape, radio, e-mail, lists, push media, mail reflectors, fax, podcasts, webcast
			briefing, newsletters
Bi Directional	telephone calls	face-to-face, conversations, telephone calls	letters, e-mail, videomail, voicemail
	web conferencing	web conferencing	reflector, mailings, forum, threading, blog
	books, speeches, mass media	audio conferencing, multipoint conferencing, party lines	briefing, training

Table IV.4. Examples of communication forms *

The Future

When assessing current trends, it is reasonable to expect that one of the main players in the CRM space will develop fully integrated software that can integrate many of the above mentioned tools into a single system within twelve to eighteen months. I make this projection based upon the growth of acceptance and use of said tools. With a variety of devices in hand such as the cellular telephone, PDA or PC you will be able to access the tools. Organizations that

* Picture IV.4. Provide by Ronald Plompen, Flyzone B.V.

fail to follow this trend will miss many opportunities that they otherwise would realize by taking advantage of them. The higher management of larger corporations will be challenged to become accustomed to using such tools simply to keep up. The days of "have your girl call my girl" and "we'll do lunch" are long past.

Conclusion

The conclusion you can draw is that all the above tools do have value in the maintenance and development of an existing network. In some cases they are absolutely vital if you have contacts across the globe with whom you want to maintain close contact. However, the personal trust relationship will always remain the basis of any solid network. This is something that definitely cannot be done solely via the use of electronic systems.

However, with the way a system such as SecondLife is developing and the new generation that is already tapping into this type of tool, we can't ignore that SecondLife may prove to be a new addition to the way one can network, or even become a completely new way.

Chapter 4
Building a Network - Do's and Don'ts

At a large Event or Seminar

Do:

- Prepare a participants' list and target those people you want to meet specifically.

- Gather as much background information as you can on the individuals you have targeted using search engines and similar tools.

- Think about what you want to offer the other party (remember - it's a "two-way-street").

- Follow up within twenty-four hours with relevant information to the person you just met. This a) shows you are genuinely interested, and b) you will still remember what it was you discussed!

- Make sure that you have something that people will remember. They are going to meet hundreds of people at this event. You want to stand out in terms of subject or enthusiasm and passion with what you have to say.

- Listening is as, if not more important, than talking.

- Dress and behave appropriately for the event.

Don't:

- Don't be a squirrel and try and gather hundreds of business cards at an event. You won't follow them up!

- Don't stalk people. Find an appropriate time to approach someone.

- Don't tell tall stories or use hyperbole. Concentrate on being truthful and sincere.

- Don't try and sell here. This is about showing interest and building a base for a future relationship.

Maintaining your network

Do:

- Try and meet in person at least once a year (individually or via your own events, golf, concerts etc.).

- Find out what people's personal interests; what makes them tick.

- On the business front, offer something new such as a newsletter, a regular e-mail update or set up a meeting on new topics.

- On a personal level, send small notes on birthdays and congratulations on personal events. It hardly matters what you send. The fact is that you are keeping in touch in some small way often enough.

- You can set up an interest IBM Lotus Sametime group, such as Advisory Boards or Expert Forums IBM Lotus Sametime. Get your contacts involved in your business.

- When people move jobs, even if this means that they are not interesting to your business, keep in touch. This is also valid with people retiring. They may still come back to do something useful. Retired people are often not out of the loop.

- Keep in touch with your ex-colleagues (the bright ones!).

Don't:

- Don't just ask, give something back.

- Never lose sight of the subtle cultural distinctions at work. East Coast is not the same as West Coast

U.S., which differs again greatly from Europe. But
equally, each industry has its own culture, and you
can even expand this to each company.

Chapter 5
OHM Inc. -
The N Factor at Work

In almost all cases networks will be applied to help a business grow and flourish and people will build a network for a very specific reason. Good examples of this are approaching wealthy individuals for private investment purposes and wealth management, or to sell a particular piece of software to a targeted area of an organization. In this way, you build a network that is related to only this purpose and activity.

When building such networks the danger is that they engender short-term relationships rather than building and nurturing long-term ones. We see that a lot of people—although they are constantly busy building a network—do this only in order to fulfill a particular, fairly limited role in a particular organization. Often, when they change roles or organizations subsequently, they do not take the trouble to maintain the relationships they already have but move on to build a new, particular network suited to their latest circumstances. In fact, this is a senseless destruction of capital invested and a great waste of time and energy.

In 2004, a number of partners including myself founded a new company called OHM Inc. In this organization, a number of elements of sound networking come together. The common denominator of all partners is that they have spent their careers networking and maintaining their individual networks; have been involved throughout in technology industries; have a background in sales; and have built and/or sold at least one company. One of the unique features of OHM is that the N Factor, applying true networking, is the very core and purpose of its business. All partners are people who have made networking into their profession.

OHM's activities are based on the leverage of contacts in the Fortune 1500 organizations on behalf of (emerging) technology companies.

As we have stated earlier, a network needs to be treated respectfully and with care. Contacts have been built and maintained over many years and the investment is worth protecting. For us to start working with a technology company, we therefore adhere to a strict, self-defined set of rules in order to make sure we also look after our contacts' interests. The client has to have a proven and working product. The company has to be funded and have at least five clients to reference (mid- to large-sized organizations). During engagement of a new client, at least two of the partners are present. Both will have to agree that the proposition is valid. During the intake, the partners together with the client will create a "wish-list" of companies that the provider would like to have as customers. This can be by geography, industry or simply companies. Upon knowing where our customer seeks introduction, we will distribute the names to all partners and advisors. Each of these will indicate where he or she has contacts. The contacts we have within a Fortune 1500 company are used solely to get to the right decision maker for the particular client with its specific product. This is a strong example of top-down introductions. During the first conversation between client and contact, one of the partners of OHM will be present to ensure that the introduction is done properly and to ensure that our carefully built network is protected. We obviously work to ensure that our clients meet the contacts they seek. We also have to make sure that the products or services we present to our contacts are of value; that something useful is delivered to their organization. We are committed to ensuring there is a win-win situation both for our clients and our contacts in which we all benefit.

As a result of our careful approach to building the bridge between our client, the technology provider, and matching them and their solution to our contacts in the Fortune 1500, we are recognized as a serious source when looking for a solution to a specific problem. Based on the trust relationship we are enjoying with our contacts, and the fact that they know we provide relevant solutions, contacts are more and more seeking us out specifically whenever they have an issue that a technology can solve.

It has absolutely proven to be an advantage to do this in a relatively young industry using what has become so much a common language, English. A lack of old school ties or political connections does not prevent one from building the network, given expenditure of the necessary effort. In this sense, technology is an integral element in conjunction with hard work and effort when building a network.

On top of that, we have been able to attract a number of highly exceptional people as advisors to our business, on the strength of our own contacts who are of high stature in their own industries. These individuals allow us to leverage their networks in turn for our clients. The fact that these advisors were prepared to align themselves in this role with OHM also had a lot to do with our strength in building long-term relationships, mutual respect, and the constant understanding that any networking has to be a two-way-street. We are always prepared to help others as they are always prepared to help us.

OHM has now been going for a couple of years and is extremely successful. It has been cash flow positive from the start and grows by over 100 percent per year. OHM has proven to be an excellent basis from which to launch new initiatives. As the concept seems relatively simple, a lot of people believe that this is easily done and can be copied.

However, they forget that this is based on a whole generation's worth of investment in relationships by each of the partners in OHM. The obligation of the partners is to constantly be alert and think about each introduction in terms of the people you introduce to each other and whether the product brought to the table is a good one for the specific contact. In short, we always consider *what's in it for them* as well as for ourselves and our clients; this is precisely what we mean by the N Factor – that indefinable extra dimension that means everyone benefits. In this way you can keep your circle of contacts fresh, interested, and intact.

Case Study

One of our clients is called NetDialog, co-founded by Jos Bourgonje – a serial entrepreneur. NetDialog's product requires introductions at a high-level in the corporate world. Jos understands as no other, that in order to get to this level fast, the very best approach is through a solid network.

"OHM offers a very structured methodology to our company, NetDialog. We want to approach our prospects top-down, because we know we have a strategic asset to offer. This cannot be done with a large quantitatively managed CRM and cold calling. We need experienced business oriented and savvy entrepreneurs to represent us and not necessarily in a fixed infrastructure with offices, locations and associated cost levels. We want our dream team to be where the business is, wherever it is.

"OHM was very proficient in understanding our

proposition so we had a quick start. They brought us valuable, world renowned prospects and more importantly, connected us with the proper decision making units. The people we met not only had a problem relevant to the context of our proposition, but had budget and willingness to work with us."

Scalability and Networking, the N Factor is key to this concept.

Chapter 6

Lifestyle

First impressions are often lasting impressions, so I want to spend some attention on clothing, behavior, choice of restaurant and so on. These factors are often dictated by local custom and can vary even from region to region.

Clothing

Although clothing is of course a highly personal choice, and a reflection of who you are as a person, small changes or a basic understanding of the country or region you want to do business in may be sufficient to help your contact run smoothly.

For example, if you go to Silicon Valley and visit technology companies, it is almost always very informal: slacks with a polo or T-shirt. It's pretty much the norm there so should you arrive in your best suit and tie, you are guaranteed to be considered "overdressed." Although nobody will hold it against you, you miss the opportunity of the first impression "he or she is one of us." Austin, Texas is fairly similar to Silicon Valley; however, Dallas, while only a short hop away, is much more formal and the informal dress code of Silicon Valley and Austin would be slightly frowned upon there.

New York's dress code is more formal when you visit financial institutions and a bit more informal when talking to tech companies. New York is also the place of "Casual Friday" – although this is becoming less common. I still find it difficult to guess what should be worn in New York. When visiting this city, I used to turn up in a suit when everyone was wearing casual and the other way round. These days, I ask what the dress code of the company I'm visiting is so I can adjust...safer to ask!

Europe is different again than the U.S. Europeans are in general, more formal, particularly when you are visiting the large corporations and most certainly when you are visiting financials in London. Even in Amsterdam—known for its casual approach to many things—you are expected to dress formally, meaning suit and tie or equivalent for ladies. In Europe, your safest bet is to dress up instead of dress down.

Dressing well does not always have to mean you have to dress expensively. These days, even large chains carry good suits designed by the top designers.

Another thing that comes to mind on the topic of Clothing is the time a Dutch bank acquired a UK Bank.

The British press had a field day writing about the fact that the Dutch wore brown shoes under their blue suit. This just serves to show that small things are important. Better to check and know what goes in certain cultures, than to assume it won't matter once they have gotten to know you.

Restaurants

If you invite someone for dinner in a restaurant, the question always crops up – which restaurant to choose? Although it would perhaps seem obvious, even a five star restaurant is not always the solution. The art of choosing the restaurant is to choose one that will pleasantly surprise your guest and allow you to achieve your objective.

If you know the assistant of your guest, it is worthwhile asking what type of food your contact actually likes, what cuisine he prefers or even which foods he specifically does not like. It helps tremendously in narrowing down the choices and you can avoid the classic mistake of taking a vegetarian to the best steakhouse in town.

Some other examples:

Although trendy can be fun, it is usually a younger person who is most interested in going to these types of restaurants.

A growing group of people is interested in wines (U.S. and certainly in Europe) so find a restaurant renowned for its wine list/cellar.

The other element you should consider is the atmosphere. Do you want loud and noisy, or do you want to hold a decent conversation? This may be a tricky one to get right – hotspots, especially in the big cities such as New York and London are often not the quietest places.

All of these things are important to take into account, particularly if you work across the globe. Use local people's knowledge to find out what is good or not at that time, don't rely just on your own past experiences. A restaurant may have changed hands between your last time there and now...

If you plan on carrying on after dinner, make sure you plan this as carefully as the rest of the evening. Take care to reserve a place somewhere that fits the occasion and your guest. Trawling from place to place, being rejected at the door is one sure way of making sure you ruin an evening even if it started out superbly with the dinner you booked. I once took a U.S. guest to the Lido in Paris. And although this is an excellent show, tastefully done and not sleazy at all, it shocked my guest more than I had anticipated. Equally, I was once taken by a New York banker to a small club where they held a transvestite show and although I thought it was good fun, it is not something that you could just take anyone to, certainly not if this is the first time you plan an evening. On another occasion we were invited to lunch with some-one we had never met before, but to whom we were intro-duced by a mutual acquaintance. On arrival at the lunch venue it turned out to be a cigar bar, where one could also sit down for lunch. For a non-smoker, this is not a very attractive proposition at the best of times but given that I was suffering badly from a bout of hay fever at the time I felt like I was being choked to death. This meeting never resulted in further business opportunities, someone who is not considerate enough to know the tastes or distastes of his invitees, will never be a considerate partner in business either.

One final word of warning: even if the evening is great, the food excellent and your guest superbly happy, drinking too much is not an option. One can never make as good an impression drunk as when you are sober. And most people do not improve much after a few (too many) drinks. They tend to think they are being extremely funny and witty, but often the reverse is the case.

The same is true for in-flight "entertainment." This is one of those places where you often see people who have had a few drinks, perhaps to calm their nerves or pass the time. They invariably end up annoying their fellow passengers. So while travel is a great way to meet new people, it is not people who overly drink that end up with the great contacts.

On the whole, being healthy and fit is important when you are working hard and travelling frequently. I am all for a healthy lifestyle: no smoking, not too much alcohol, and doing some form of sport regularly. Almost all major hotels have health clubs these days. And guess what? This is another excellent location to meet people with like-minded interests!

When I was preparing for the New York Marathon I would always take my shoes with me and go out running three to four times a week. I am still in touch with various people I met while running on a treadmill in a hotel and we agreed to run together when I next met them. In the meantime, we have established an excellent business understanding and relationship and all because of this one thing we have in common, running.

Chapter 7
Networking in Politics

Networking in politics is something that is not the first thing that comes to mind when people talk about Social Networking. That is not necessarily the case since networking often happens in the closed inner circles of politics where it is indeed a very essential skill to have.

In January 2007, the Dutch government was being formed after general elections held in November of 2006. This requires a building of trust between the different parties with their often very different visions on a particular topic. Networking is an important factor in building a mutual foundation for the coalition to be based on.

Informal networks can be essential to a politician to get the right coalition government, or the approval of new laws.

Since we feel that political networking is important to the completeness of our book and we have little experience of it ourselves, we have asked Jake Siewert, former press secretary of former President Bill Clinton to gives us a view on networking in U.S. politics, which adds an interesting insight to the use of the N Factor in a different manner the that in business.

As Networking is not just an item in U.S. politics, but an art that has been practiced over the centuries all over the world, we have also asked an insider, Mr. Zsolt Szabo—former member of the Dutch government party VVD—to give us a glimpse of what goes on behind the closed doors of Dutch politics.

It does not mean that we approve and align ourselves necessarily with Zsolt's political views, but they are essential to this chapter and we have therefore left the original material as complete as possible.

Networking in U.S. Politics

By Jake Siewert, VP Global Communications, Alcoa

In Washington political circles, the word "network" is often used to describe a more benign form of "lobbying," a time-honored activity in the nation's Capitol. One derivation of the word "lobbyist," perhaps apocryphal, dates back to the post-Civil War era when President Grant would stroll from the White House over to the Willard Hotel lobby for his afternoon cocktail. Those seeking to influence him and the course of reconstruction funding would linger in the lobby of the Willard and wait for a chance to make their case to the president, presumably after he had finished a drink or two.

Today, the Willard lobby is busier than ever, the number of lobbyists has sky-rocketed, and modern presidents don't walk the streets of Washington. But much of today's political networking and lobbying still transpires over cocktails and meals. As the White House and Congress empty out in the evening, bars and restaurants on Capitol Hill, DuPont Circle, Georgetown and K Street fill up with politicos who want to share a beer and the latest behind-the-scenes news.

Time pressure has greatly reduced other opportunities for networking in DC. The first White House staff meeting typically starts at 7 AM. Those who gather in the Roosevelt Room are expected to have digested the morning papers and prepared responses to the overnight news. Lunch is mostly eaten at a desk not a table, and it is a rare evening when the staff leaves before 7:30 PM. During a crisis - and the White House is almost always in the middle of some crisis - the days are considerably longer on both ends. Congressional staff show up for work later, but votes are regularly scheduled between 8 PM and midnight. Reporters who cover politics have to deal with later deadlines, and Internet and cable news that literally never stops.

By lengthening the daily media cycle, the explosion of the Internet and cable TV has made the Washington workday longer for everyone. With those long days, the hours after work—between 8 and 10 **PM**—offer one of the few times for those in the media, politics, think tanks, and lobbying to interact. An early game of tennis or an afternoon of golf are not viable options in the non-stop political culture in DC. Blackberries and cell phones allow people to keep in touch during the day, but aren't ideal for the kind of personal back-and-forth that is critical in politics. So, don't expect to bump into the president at the bars at Willard or Occidental today. But, around 9:30 **PM** after the tourists have gone to bed, drop in to the bar at Hay Adams across the street from the White House - or The Monocle behind the Senate offices - and you are likely to see some high-powered politicians huddled at a table, catching up, making a deal, and just maybe having a drink.

The Use of The N Factor in Dutch Politics.

By Zsolt Szabo

Zsolt Szabo was a member of Dutch Parliament between 2003 and 2006. Prior to this, Zsolt performed various activities for Members of Parliament while reading political science in the eighties and has therefore gained experience of Networking in Politics both in the pre-technology era and today.

In 2002, shortly before the national elections, the popular Dutch politician Pim Fortuyn was shot and killed by an environmental activist. The result of this killing created a true political earthquake; the effects of which can be felt up until today. Nothing remained the same in The Hague, the political capital of the Netherlands. Parliaments come and go at a speed more familiar to Italy and the public's vote is shifting from one party to another, moving away from their previously steadfast choices. One could ask whether networking in such an unstable political environment is even worth doing.

From the foundation of modern-day Dutch democracy in 1848 up to 2002, the ways of Parliament have been nothing but "traditional:" fixed processes, traditional means such as pen and paper and a tightly hierarchical political culture based on respect for the senior, experienced leaders. The ability to gain and maintain relevant contacts (the N Factor) in order to achieve your political goals, has been applied very differently post 2002 than before.

Traditional networking used to be very organized: a good cigar, a stiff drink in the club and meeting each other in person from time to time in order to catch up on various issues. However, since the 2002 elections, two-thirds of the then Members of Parliament have left and been replaced by new, young and inexperienced politicians. The exodus of the previous group of politicians has therefore also meant a change of generation. The three-piece suited, cigar smoking, traditionally minded group has been replaced by a generation mostly in its thirties and forties with none of the old and hierarchical modus operandi.

There is another significant difference with the pre-2002 leaders and that is the ease with which the new group uses computers and other technology. An example was a live TV show, at a time when computers were not as commonly used by politicians as they are today, in which our former Prime Minister Mr. Wim Kok (1994-2002) showed that he was not totally comfortable with computers.

Take in comparison Mr. Kok's successor, Mr Balkenende who communicates twenty-four hours a day via his Blackberry with all the members of his party. And see the connectivity of all Members of Parliament via mobile, computer and the latest tools. They are now being supported by a full IT department especially implemented to assist the 150 people, large group of politicians, in the houses of Parliament. At the end of this chapter we'll have a look at the use of modern communication tools and how they are applied in politics.

The precise definition of what is understood by the creation and maintenance of relevant contacts for political purposes is no doubt different for each Member of Parliament. Each of them is in fact an entrepreneur, of course operating within the domain of their own political party but nevertheless aiming at optimizing their own output. This means that each of them has their own agenda, be it in the open or hidden, with their future careers and income as the primary goal. You can consider there being two types of representatives of the public, as far as these careers go: One being those counselors coming from the local government ranks, who have as their principal aim before and after their spell in Parliament a political and governmental career; and those counselors that come from the world of business and wish to add something extra to politics based on their business backgrounds so that politics can continue to reflect a realistic image of our society.

Due to this duplicity, one can see many different ways of networking, connecting and intersecting each other. Those that strive for a governmental career, mostly use networking to create safety nets. Once they leave politics, they wish to find themselves in another leading governmental role. This is, in fact, a very defensive way of networking aimed at the consolidation of their work environment.

This being in contrast to the real entrepreneurs in politics, who tend to network mostly externally and see a possible opportunity in each new contact they encounter. The latter type of networking is more offensive, done taking greater risk and using greater courage. The interesting aspect of this observation is the fact that quite naturally these two types of representatives will remain secluded from each other and that they do not network with the other group unless forced to do so in order to achieve common goals.

During the time I acted as a Member of Parliament, I was spokesperson for the policy areas of IT, Defense and Development Cooperation. Of course, I have been lobbied intensively by the groups covered under these policy areas. Here you also see the earlier mentioned difference between the more governmental types versus entrepreneurs. Lobbying done by the IT and defense industries could not be more different than that of the development agencies.

In all three cases I dealt with professionals, meaning these people were employed by and earning an income from their activities. That, however, was at the same time the only thing they had in common. Both the IT and Defense lobbyists' purpose is to sell goods and services with the single goal of generating revenue and profits while the lobby for charitable purposes was made up of semi-government officials who had been subsidized for many years by the State. Their, often hidden, agenda is only to continue their activities and increase this subsidy year after year with the agreement of Parliament but without a single commitment to achieving any type of result.

Because of the strong intertwining of government and development agencies one can speak here of one large single network of government officials and agencies against the politicians. A further observation is that a part of the spokespeople of the developmental agencies came from those very same agencies. As a skeptical politician in this policy area, I therefore started my term 2-0 behind, which I used to my advantage in my networking strategy. My goal was to finally question non-performance and support of future goals of the development lobby. The first months in office, I saw scores of lobbyists claiming that the development agencies had achieved phenomenal successes. My reply was that they had in reality achieved hardly anything at all, and that I no longer wished to speak with them as it was of zero value. I was able to present my ideas about how you could in fact achieve far better cooperation on development of the third world via often confrontational discussions with directors of development agencies using TV, radio, gatherings and frequent direct contact with the leading official in question. I shied away on purpose from the normal, typical "The Hague" method of massaging and taking small steps at a time. Instead I sought the more confrontational route. Within existing agencies and organizations this did little to generate friendships in the first instance, but I now often hear that due to this direct approach they did start to think about and revise significantly their policies in order to achieve a much better and successful cooperation with the business world.

The old-fashioned, finely balanced and geared-toward-compromise network patterns have frustrated the output of governmental policy for far too long. Every one has been too secure in his position and has been able to fend off intruders who were of a different mind by avoiding discussion about truly long-term economical success. Those successes unfortunately do not exist! There are in fact many examples of economic growth in African countries being stunted and corruption allowed at worst, or stimulated at best by such so called Development Cooperation initiatives.

Although unorthodox, my approach, and even if it went directly against existing and accepted methods of political communication, has proven to be effective. This has to do with the Netherlands as it is post 2002. However, the true test is to gain an advance in years to come after the shake-up of the officials in The Hague. I have therefore put a lot of energy in the upcoming generation of politicians who will in their future roles be the ones to form and renew our policies. This also is very much part of networking, laying the grounds for long-term renewal.

In contrast to those examples such as for instance Ayaan Hirsi Ali—who knew very well how to start the process of agitation but did not know how to then follow up and bed things down in a new pattern—I have exerted myself towards the (future) policymakers to accept and adopt those suggested policy changes so that my ideas will not fade away once I have ended my term.

To give you one further example on the Defense lobby, as spokesperson for Defense I was responsible on behalf of my party (which was part of the then government) for the JSF dossier. The JSF dossier was based on the question whether or not the Netherlands should purchase new fighter jets as a replacement of the F-16s the Netherlands still used. In this complex environment, one can identify two types of networking besides that of the Ministry itself. One was the lobby from the defense-industry and the other my own towards the opposition in order to gain the support needed for the acquisition of the fighter jets. Foreign gentlemen presented their material and tried to influence their own national politicians in order to in turn influence the Dutch. I myself had become convinced of the need to purchase the JSF at an early stage and therefore did not focus on the functionality of the jet itself but rather on the many opportunities offered to the advancement of the Dutch knowledge state. Bringing production and maintenance activities to the Netherlands would have an obvious positive impact on employment in our country. The left opposition in the Netherlands who was against the acquisition of the JSF but of course in favor of increases in employment and further generation of our knowledge economy, therefore in the end were not able to come up with a better counter-argument than the eternal "I am against because I am against", which obviously held no value.

In the case of the development agency wanting to con-solidate their failing policies further, I confronted the net-work of those in charge head on – while in the other case, that of the JSF dossier, I avoided the discussion on the qual-ities of the fighter jet itself and focused on building a net-work which would support the desire to build on our knowl-edge economy – and was therefore an industry all too pleased to help and support my case. In both of these situ-ations, the choice of how to apply networking proved there-fore to be successful.

From now on, Development cooperation is account-able for its achievements and the JSF has been ordered which will benefit Dutch industry optimally.

To utilize the N Factor, in political terms defined as "the ability to build and maintain relevant contacts in order to achieve one's political goals, optimally," one has to be able and willing to play on multiple chess boards simultaneously as well as needing to be able to stay a few moves ahead of your opponent. In reality this is not very different from networking in the earlier days. However, in my view it has to be achieved at a completely different speed and partially under pressure from the new media. The media these days force politicians to have well-formulated opinions one tenth of a second after Reuters, ANP or other newswires have issued a politically relevant news item. In comparison to the past, where news slowly filtered out and the politician had the time to formulate a careful answer after the news had been verified, news these days is available immediately – whether it makes sense or not. As debates between members of Parliament are often fought in the public eye and less physically inside the Parliament buildings – the production of political news is shifting from inside those buildings to outside the house of Parliament.

As mentioned at the start of this chapter, Dutch politics is still feeling the aftershocks of the earthquake that hit it in 2002. The Dutch political climate has become and continues to become more and more uncertain. As a result of the greater turnover of politicians who are one year nominated as "Politician of the Year" only to be nominated the next year for the "Worst Politician," it can be concluded that to be in possession of whichever factor you can think of, offers less guarantees for success in the long term than in the world of business where one also faces quakes and aftershocks but where the measuring apparatus is better equipped to measure these shocks and anticipate them. This does not take away from the relevance and importance of the N Factor. However, this N Factor is more and more dependent on the combination of a feeling for the political game and the ability to face the daily bombardments of information fired at politicians.

The intensity of these bombardments will only increase over time. The challenge is to make the right selection of news combined with maintaining an excellent relationship with the press on the one hand and reaching sound agreements, if possible, with your own coalition partners and the opposition on the other hand. This purely so that you maintain some control over your own political agenda. And since 2002 politics is more difficult to direct, politicians will have to learn to cope with the coincidence factor while networking which means that one is constantly confronted with the expression of the media whose content is harder to anticipate upfront.

Consistency of political expressions ought to be rewarded at the end of the day with gaining seats in Parliament, as it did pre-2002. If this will happen is the big question. Possibly one will have to introduce another factor that plays a role on the political stage – the U-factor, U reflecting the margin of Uncertainty.

Let's come back to the use of modern technology in networking in politics. Before the computer-era, all communication was done necessarily face-to-face, via telephone or post. The introduction of computers, mobile phones and PDA's has merely extended the range of possible communication methods. It is important though to reflect on the increase in speed achieved by these tools, among other factors, has led to "real-time politics" – when something happens, it is known all over the world instantly. Another important change that has crept in over recent years is the fear of leakages. Whereas one used to be concerned about holding confidential conversations via telephone as one did not know who might be listening in, these days even a private conversation is no guarantee for a safe discussion. This is due to the advance of technology, including recording functionalities in phones or webcams.

The use of modern communication tools also has a large number of positive effects. As distraction or in some cases addiction, more politicians appear to hook up to (online) games. These games are particularly popular during long debates and voting ceremonies. On a more serious note – it offers members of Parliament the possibility to send each other information immediately, much more quickly than the use of envelopes which had to be taken to another member via messengers which often resulted in the relevant topic having been dealt with before the information even reached the recipient.

Worth noting is that most of these communications which politicians send each other are serious in content, but often accompanied by a joke or quip. Take a seat in the public area to follow these bilateral exchanges between members of Parliament and congress and you will note that despite the weight and seriousness of the debate, politicians also manage to have a lot of fun.

As a member of the committee for technology policy and member of strategic direction regarding IT in the Chamber, I have always been an advocate of the modernization of the communication and information channels in Parliament. There have been many debates about the changes that had to be made in order to allow laptops in the plenary chamber and facilities for online voting, both in the Chamber and remotely. The result has been that all these technological support systems will be implemented in Parliament over the coming years. Possibly the voting remotely by Members of Parliament will lead to some resistance, but the fact that members often have to wait unnecessarily for many hours to vote, and thereby miss opportunities for speaking engagements "in the field" is no longer of this day and age. However, the decision process in politics is often very slow and tedious. For instance, in The Hague, the House only meets between Tuesday and Thursday. The reason for this was that historically, Members of Parliament used to come to The Hague by horse-drawn carriages. During the weekends they had to be seen locally going to church; this only left Mondays and Fridays for travel.

It is quite likely that those against voting remotely will argue that Members of Parliament will never turn up in The

Hague anymore. However, my observation is that members are professional enough and wise enough to find a fitting way to deal with the issue of both being seen and attending sessions in The Hague and attending events elsewhere. The earthquake rocking Dutch politics in 2002 has proven that politicians do not merely need to network in The Hague, but also, and certainly not least importantly – in the country among their voters.

Chapter 8
So Many Countries, So Many Cultures

To provide a greater context for the N Factor from a cultural perspective, it is necessary to give a bit of background on my networking in and with a variety of cultures. Even though I was born and raised in the Netherlands, I met with other cultures early on in my life. My very first experience with a different culture to the one in which I was born into was during my childhood. My family moved to Indonesia for two years. Perhaps this is what gave me my interest in, and taste for, living and working in other countries.

During my career, I have always had an affinity for dealing with other cultures and have done business in a diverse range of locations. For one of my companies I had an exclusive distributorship with an Italian company, representing them in the Benelux. For my technology companies, I had subsidiaries in Spain, the UK, Germany, Belgium and the

U.S. I have done acquisitions in Germany, UK, Brazil and the U.S. and I have dealt with VC's in the Netherlands, Germany, France and the UK. This has all taken place over the course of the past thirty years, so my view on networking is definitely very global. It has also allowed me to better understand the different cultures. Living in the U.S. has enabled me with a more profound insight into the American culture. You soon understand that this is very different from flying somewhere, doing business there and then returning to your home country. When you travel to a foreign country only to do business sometimes the only way you know you are in a different country is because the taxi driver is speaking a language you don't understand.

The danger of the "in-and-out" approach is that you may think you understand the culture in question. The fact that you speak their language (mostly English), or the Marriott you stay at looks exactly like the one in your country and because all offices look the same you believe that you also understand the person in this culture and the way he/she thinks.

Not so! For example, in some cultures it is just not considered appropriate to say "no." However, this does not mean they just told you "yes." Someone may say "this is interesting" which you interpret as meaning they would like to continue, whereas you have really just been told they are not going to have anything to do with it. One culture may be very direct, whereas in another one, you may need the patience and tact of a diplomat.

From this perspective, we thought it would be valuable and interesting to add a number of different contributions from well-known business people in various corners of the world. Not because we want to state that this is a complete overview of the various cultures you may ever deal with, but more to underline the fact that there are great differences between the various countries. When you are networking in a different country, take time to research and understand the culture that you will be working with. Be respectful of your contact's culture or else all you will ever achieve will be a very short-term and casual relationship, at best. Use all your knowledge and research in these cases to create that extra dimension, the N Factor.

It was interesting to see, from the contributions that follow below what differences exist between the various cultures as far as networking is concerned. However, what is ultimately more interesting is the similarities that are revealed.

Time after time, it appears that the binding factor, the N Factor, central to the networks you build over the long term are the people themselves, not the company you or they represent or the background they may have. Of course education, their history, and so on play a role, in particular when you first meet, but over a longer period of time it is essentially the chemistry between people which determines whether you can build a strong, trust relationship even at a business level.

Vision on the N Factor in the East Coast, U.S.

By Steve Etzler

I founded Business Development Institute in 2001 as a networking organization. Our mission was to connect business development executives with each other. Networking at its very core, is about how to get to know people. It doesn't really matter if the purpose is for business or friendships. The reality is there are lots of people we don't know that we want to know to enrich both our personal and professional lives. The fundamental lesson I have learned is business is about people dealing with people, not companies dealing with companies or consumers. People, not companies, sign contracts. People evaluate and judge each other, companies don't. The most important common denominator for any successful relationship is trust. It doesn't matter if we are discussing marriage, friendships or business. Everything is based on trust. The challenge is how to start a new relationship with someone we don't know so we can establish mutual trust.

The simplest rule I follow is to do things I promise to do. It's absolutely amazing that people meet each other and talk about all the things they want to do. Next steps are outlined and agreed upon. Then people start dropping balls everywhere. If you want to start a new relationship on the right foot, do something that you promise you will do. I know this sounds like basic common sense, but again, people constantly drop the ball when following up after the initial meeting.

The next rule is to focus on how you can help the other person first. Many look at new business relationships as how the other person can help you. We all know that relationships are a two-way-street. Put aside what you want from a relationship and focus on the needs of the other person. Go out of your way to meet those needs. It helps establish trust and the other person will be much more willing to in turn, help you. It will also enhance your reputation as someone who is a *good guy* or a *good girl* that's not only out for himself/herself.

Vision on the N Factor in China

By Evelyn Lee

Whereas Western business cultures tend to be transaction-oriented and seemingly impersonal at times, Chinese business culture is mainly relationship-oriented. A complete and working formula for networking effectively in China is connection with mutual obligation, goodwill, and personal affection with special emphasis placed on family and shared experiences (such as college and military service).

How does networking work in China?

For a foreign company with no existing network connections in China that is considering entering into the Chinese market, hiring overseas Chinese citizens to serve as a bridge for Westerners to access the Chinese market would be a valuable option to consider.

If you are traveling to and planning on doing business in China, your circle of friends should ideally be introducing you to their connections or contacts. Usually, you will be asked to convey a positive greeting to your new contact, and the more elaborate the greeting, the closer and more friendly the contact is expected to be with you. For example, a written letter with a handwritten signature would represent one of the more serious introductions, and is viewed as the foundation for a stronger relationship to be built upon.

Chinese people have a very different mind-set when compared to the peoples of most other countries. Therefore, it is very difficult for a foreign company to develop their own network in China without gaining the assistance via referral of Chinese acquaintances, partners or employees. Besides seeking a referral by Chinese acquaintances, the company should visibly be seeking a strategic Chinese partner or partners, and/or be hiring reliable and resourceful Chinese employees who have existing wide networks. These are the keys to gaining access in the Chinese market.

It is important to understand that networks are formed among individuals with interpersonal relationships and not simply "with companies." When a person moves on from a position of employment, their replacement will of course not automatically inherit the network; their personal connections go with them. Sometimes companies will appoint the new person far in advance so that the replacement can be introduced to the existing network and form their own relationships. So if you are dealing with a Chinese company, it is worthwhile to develop your network beyond only one or a few individuals. If your point person were to leave the company, your account would probably be assumed by a replacement, and you may not find yourself in the same standing.

How does someone make the right kind of contacts and maintain them in China?

To create a working and positive contact for a specific business, ask other experienced and effective people in that field to refer you. Referral is of course important because it represents trust, especially in China.

For a foreign company, you also have to be able to demonstrate that you are capable in specific fields, such that you would have enough strength in your own business to realize a deal with another company that thinks your strength is useful in developing their interest as well. Building effective and lasting business relationships founded on trust is a must.

For the Chinese, the giving of symbolic or representational gifts can help to strengthen the relationship in a whole new way. The gift should be something that either considers the recipient's personal or specific interests or that is a symbol of your own personal background, such as something from your own hometown. The gift should not be expensive, as something too costly would be too difficult to reciprocate. Even without meaning to, it could therefore embarrass the recipient as it could be hard for them to return the favor.

To maintain healthy and working network relationships, a steady exchange of communication and favors should be maintained. Favors should be repaid with slightly larger ones, but not anything too much larger or it will not represent a natural strengthening of the relationship and will seem posed.

A healthy interest in the family of your network partner helps to build and maintain the relationship. While Westerners often consider their family lives to be separate from their business ones, the Chinese do not draw this distinction, creating closer ties within the entire social structure seemingly. As such, the Chinese frequently exhibit family-like behavior in business settings. Asking about their parents, remembering their children's birthdays, and sending gifts to them help to build and maintain the relationship.

How do I know I am in a good network?

It is a good idea to verify the person's reputation. Testing them with something small first is generally a wise idea. Keep in mind that a network relationship with somebody who has a bad reputation can lock you out of other networks simply through word of mouth.

What to do and what not to do?

The methods mentioned in maintaining the contacts are the right thing to do, such as providing good dinner, or sending festival greetings which can maintain a close or at least stable relationship with your network person. When there is a good deal, Chinese people tend to come to think of the persons involved as having a closer relationship with them due to the shared successes.

Try especially to show respect to your network person and not to embarrass them.

How to expand the network and business?

The most important way to expand the network is to have your own strength and capacity. Deals are likely to be made because you have the strength in some specific field which they do not. One can develop the business network by strategic partnership or employing people with good networks themselves that will lend benefit to the group as a result. But be aware that China is a large country and different provinces have their own regional characteristics. So it is very hard to depend on one person and obtain the nation wide business strength in China.

Network relationships often result in favors that are expected to be returned, but by no specific date. Interestingly enough, sometimes indebtedness from such favors lasts for generations, and the Chinese will remember for a long time a favor that was given to them, especially when it was needed. When a favor is returned, it often is in greater measure. This swinging of the balance strengthens the network relationship and carries it into the future. So do not refuse to provide help if it is possible for you and you might be paid back in the long run.

When meeting people, Westerners tend to ask someone about their profession. The Chinese, however, tend to ask where you are from and then may ask if you would know somebody whom they may also know there. Such questions are intended to determine whether there is perhaps a preexisting connection.

Quite a bit of goodwill can be generated if a close friend or relative of yours lived in the hometown of the person you are getting to know. While such commonalities are enjoyed by Westerners, for the Chinese they can be the basis of a very close network relationship, due to the basic common ground being offered. If you do not have such commonalities, simply showing interest in the background of your acquaintance can show you care and can help develop the relationship as friends and partners in business!

Vision on the N Factor in France

By Marc Ravels

Probably one of the most interesting countries to observe on the phenomena of networking is France. Who says France, says networking. This sounds odd for a country that is reputed for its hierarchical model, where decisions are made at the top. Indifferent if we are talking administration or business community, isn't it the boss who decides?

The reason networking is so important is precisely because of that hierarchical structure of French society. If all decisions would really travel up to and down from the summit, as it should be according to the rules, the result would be a static, slow, and impersonal environment. Networking is the oil that enables the participants, whether individuals or entities, to move, to get things done, to come to results within decent timeframes.

Centuries of centralism have greatly contributed to the necessity of networking. As all decisions are taken in Paris, the "province" is always in waiting for the instructions from the capital. This is true for the thick-layered administration, but also for business life. French corporations are by definition headquartered in Paris. A regional office, let alone a subsidiary somewhere in the countryside, are under constant surveillance of the nerve-centre in the Light City.

On top of that, it is inconceivable that these subsidiaries communicate directly with each other; the information stream is controlled by and passes through the Parisian strongholds. Happily, this—at least in theory—suffocating system is counterbalanced by networking. To be successful, each civil servant and each manager, has to make use of his personal network vertically, within his chain of reporting, but also horizontally spread over the several divisions and scattered locations of his organization. Cutting red tape is essential. Without an efficient network, a manager cannot influence the course of actions, speed up decisions, or make his views known. In short, you cannot make a career without a network.

But also at the top, where it is very lonely due to the hierarchical command chain, *le patron* or *les grands directeurs* need their personal network of friends and supporters at all levels of the organization, to obtain reliable feedback on their actions, to know their popularity rate, and to learn the real issues that remain coveted by their subordinates.

Last but definitely not least the intertwining of public and private interests, the close relations—and dependencies—of public and private administration, create networks automatically.

An entrepreneur, either commanding a small or a big entity, will never act without keeping the public authorities abreast of current and future developments of his enterprise. A regular visit to the local mayor, the *préfet* (governor) or the minister is part of his charter. He is proud of his good relationship with the municipality, province *(département)* or the State, and considers the interest of civil servants or elected members for his company as an encouragement to his business acumen.

Public interest is by definition among the "stake holding" of any company; whether or not (local) government holds shares is of limited relevance, as any company will be cautious not to alienate the public powers. A phone call from a ministry has sometimes more impact than the deliberations of the board of directors. The other way around this is also true; the business community counts on the active support from the administration and the political parties where French "strategic" interests are at stake. The interpretation of "strategic" is rather flexible, and includes most likely many more sectors than would be considered strategic by other countries.

The creation of a network in France is basically not very different from other countries: personal contacts, introductions, recommendations, home address, sports, clubs, holiday patterns etc. and yes, family. Not family in the strict sense, but as relatives. In France a family consists of many, many stakes. A far uncle or cousin whose bloodline can hardly be traced will never refrain from a little support if requested.

The originality of the French system is that there are

also citizens who are invested with networks. They don't build their network; they *automatically* gain their network if they are admitted to one of the elitist schools.* If successful, they will soon belong to the happy few with tremendous career perspectives, and be part of a powerful network, probably more powerful than in any other country. Of course, old boys systems exist in each society, in each country, but usually they provide social status and prestige to outsiders, and camaraderie and value-sharing to peers, but turn seldom into efficient professional networks.

In France on the contrary these old boys networks are extremely efficient; the fact that one has graduated at the same school provides the ticket to direct access to any other old boy, irrespective of age or position, whether in administration, in the business community or in politics. This direct access is a unique feature in the hierarchical society of France. A phone call will always be answered, a request for a rendezvous will never be denied; each and every fellow-graduate is accessible, whatever his year of graduation, position or his responsibilities. This also means the normally inaccessible persons at the top, thus surpassing all hierarchical barriers.

The top-schools prepare for the top positions. Irrespective of the administration, public corporates or private corporates, graduates of a handful of schools will be the leaders in all these domains. Careers are usually achieved at

* These schools are a kind of specialized institutes, enjoying a far higher standing than French universities. Usually after very competitive high schools, students spend some years in preparatory schools before enrolling in the—again very competitive—admission rounds at the age of twenty to twenty-two.

great speed. Undoubtedly, equally skilled but not top-school educated middle and senior management will be overtaken. Only those that went to the *grandes écoles* have access to, and will achieve, the very top of their chosen professions.

Among these prestigious schools are HEC and Essec (both business administration), Centrale (mathematics), and *Normale Superieure* (Litterature, philosophy). The most reputed of all are undoubtedly the *Ecole Nationale d'Administration* (ENA, public administration) and the *Ecole Polytechnique* (physics, engineering).

Enarques (graduates of the ENA) can be found at all the top positions in the political, public and corporate arena: presidents, prime ministers, ministers, prestigious civil servants, and CEOs. Their names are in the alumni book of the ENA. *Enarques* start their career in public administration, and can continue for the benefit of serving the highest good in France: *l'interest public.* A change to a political career follows the same logic of serving the public cause. However, quite a few *enarques* will eventually be tempted by higher pay and step into the less prestigious but financially more rewarding business life, in either publicly or privately held companies. Apart from all their knowledge and skills, their most prestigious asset is their old boys network.

Vision on the N Factor in Japan

By Mitsuyo Uchida, President, Util Holdings Inc.

A joke about Japanese people got around a few years ago. When the Titanic was about to sink, the Captain had only a limited number of boats to allocate. He wanted to make sure mainly children, ladies, and elderly people got in these, so in order to ensure that as few male adults as possible would try and use the boat, the Captain put the following to the men: To the English he said, "Dive into the sea to prove you are a true English gent." To the Americans he said, "Dive into the sea. You will be a hero". And finally to the Japanese he said, "Dive into the sea. Everybody else is doing so."

The joke pointed out a Japanese characteristic very well, namely that Japanese people are very comfortable doing the same thing others do. Japanese people have a culture in which they prefer to consider others' behaviors and preserving a spirit of harmony over asserting their own opinions. Social networking in Japan is also based on this kind of *groupism.* As Japan is an island nation and a homogeneous country, it had less opportunity to communicate and interact with different cultures than other nations in the past. In this sense, Japan is different from the western nations—who had many contacts with various races, religions, and cultures over eras of time—and it is even different from other Asian nations as well. Japanese people tend to put priority on the procedure of ceremony when they are in contact with newcomers. On the other hand, once the group has been clearly established, they may easily create a friendly but extremely tensionless society consisting purely of verbal agreements. In such a society, as the concept of contract is very weak, it is rarely defined what to do precisely. You will find this only gradually through the communication with others.

Historically, the nation of Japan was unified by Tokugawa government about 400 years ago after the Age of Civil Wars. The long and peaceful period called "Edo period" had been achieved only by a closed-door policy, which prohibited any contact with overseas countries. Practical politics was entrusted to each local lord called "Han" (domain), and any direct interference to Tokugawa government was very rare. The day-to-day life of Japanese people was operated within each Han. For samurai (warrior), Han, to whom he belonged, was the most important place, and he regarded Tokugawa government as a dangerous body and a common enemy for samurais because it had an authority to abolish Han. In the same way, his neighbor Han was also a common enemy for him. If he went out of the small world, Han, he couldn't survive, and therefore, the sense of belonging to Han was spread to all samurais. The action guideline for those people was how to avoid being disliked by Han they belonged to. The same could be applied to farmers and merchants. For them, the guideline was how to avoid being disliked by the village or town they belonged to.

After the Meiji Restoration, when Han was abolished and new unified nation as Nihon (Japan) started, the corporation was regarded as the new place to belong. This perception became stronger especially after World War II.

It is a feature of Japanese society that the credits of individuals are secured by the place they belong to. In this sense, venture business is like a masterless samurai (a maverick and unknown individual), and outstanding skill and energy shall be necessary in order to be accepted by others. Instead, once being accepted by a power elite, it could expand its networking by utilizing introductions of the power elite. Most entrepreneurs, therefore, started their steps by making approaches to such power elites or were discovered by such supporters.

When I entered this industry about twenty-five years ago, there was a Japanese ceremony of exchanging business cards, which used to surprise all foreign guests coming to Japan. For those guests, the Japanese culture to introduce oneself simply by means of printed material showing the company name, the company profile, the position, and so on seemed to be quite different from the western culture of expressing oneself through an impressive verbal and personal presentation. In Japan, the procedure that that allows all parties to mutually confirm the value of the place they belong to, and only then try to understand each individual character, is necessary.

After a seminar or a lecture, the organizer almost always arranges a social gathering. This is the time and place for exchanging business cards. Participants try to exchange business cards without any hesitation because they know that everybody in the party has the same values based on the theme of the seminar and every participant is already trusted by the organizer. Everybody present will collect as many cards as possible. Later on, each person will make direct contact with interesting persons they met at the seminar through telephone, letter, e-mail, and the like. in order to arrange for a business meeting. Almost all participants wear dark suits and they all look alike.

The key factors for these occasions are the company name and the position. People gather around the person of the most well-known company present. Although my company was not so famous, I might gain some advantages because of my position of President and also by my female gender.

If there is no seminar or other occasions for exchanging business cards, it is important to meet interesting persons by being introduced by your acquaintance. In this case, the standard procedure is that you kindly ask your acquaintance to make an appointment by phone, e-mail, and the like, in order to visit together at first. This is essential. Only later on can you arrange a subsequent business appointment by yourself.

The key fact in this first meeting is "who introduced you to the person;" other things such as "what do you do" or "what kind of benefit do you offer" are not important at the beginning. The most important thing is that you shall arrange the meeting through the common acquaintance between you and the person you are interested in. Even if you had a unique service or product to offer, without these steps, you are wasting your time.

There is another very important factor in the Japanese culture. That is the value of fulfilling your obligations. This value could mean that someone fulfills his obligation to his acquaintance by meeting you without any further purpose or desire to take it beyond the first meeting. Sometimes, Japanese people will meet you without any consideration of the actual business benefit. They may meet you only to honor their acquaintance, who introduced you to them. In this case, they will not always evaluate you and your business in a positive way. Further steps are even more necessary if you want to meet the person in charge of the company. In such cases, a staff member in each department will evaluate you and your business properly first.

The above-mentioned situation, however, has been changing in recent years. After the collapse of the bubble economy in the early 1990s, the lifetime employment system in Japan has been imploding and the sense of belonging and the loyalty to the company are weakening among Japanese people. Especially for the younger generations in their thirties and below, their sense of the values described above has been changing little by little. The thought that a company is not the body to entrust one's entire life to any more, is growing among Japanese people.

Networking is always very important. I would like to say, however, that the only key for success of networking must be the same in both Western and Eastern world. That is whether your business can give something that is of true value to the other party involved.

Vision on the N Factor in the UK

By John Handby

Networking in the UK has undergone quite a change in the last twenty years. When I grew up it was a world of *old boy networks* which depended essentially on where you went to school and university (much like I still understand France to be) as well as organizations like the freemasons. Being in the right network was important in getting the right jobs and making business contacts, and these networks still exist today, but in a much less important and pervasive way.

Partly, this has come about through the growth of a meritocracy, politicians such as Margaret Thatcher, and the enormous changes that have taken place in business. In terms of the last of these the UK has seen the decline of the commonwealth and the traditional trading arrangements, the decline of manufacture and the growth of new industries—particularly IT—where all the rules have changed.

The UK has followed the U.S. (not for the first time!) in the growth of a whole new generation of entrepreneurs and ways of doing business. This has led to a much more open and overt approach to networking. People now join networking organizations expressly designed to help them further their business aims and objectives. This has occurred in various disciplines, but particularly on the part of those working with technology.

In the case of CIOs, they have felt the need to network for a long time as they are in charge of the *black arts department.* Few of their colleagues have really understood the challenges they face and have simply seen IT as a huge money pit. So at one level CIOs have taken to *huddling together for warmth!* More seriously they have perceived a real value in coming together with those facing similar challenges and exchanging views and ideas. The first networking organization of this kind was established in the 1970's in the UK (Butler Cox organization) and has been followed by similar organizations, most recently CIO Connect in which they sought to take the concept a bit further. It is now true to say that, with over 200 major companies and government departments as members, being a member of CIO Connect has become the norm for senior IT executives.

In other disciplines such networking organizations tend to be less advanced. They certainly exist in HR, marketing and for CEOs. But probably the most significant one outside IT is that for the Finance Directors of the FTSE 100 companies.

Networking for young technology based companies really took off in the .com boom with organizations like First Tuesday and has now matured into a number of organizations like the Technology Futures Forum, the Chemistry Club, and the European Technology Forum. These meet together on a regular basis with speakers but very much with networking in mind. They tend to have CXOs from young technology companies and VCs plus a small scattering of CIOs. They would all love to have more involvement of CIOs but the value to them is limited.

The UK is of course culturally much closer to the U.S. and further from mainland Europe than geography would suggest. So while executives here do participate in some pan-European networking organizations, they are much more likely to look to participate in U.S. based networking organizations like the Conference Board or the Executive Board.

Vision on the N Factor in the U.S.

By Fred Kuglin

Introduction

In our world of global commerce and megacorporations, there are a few business principles that are common in every country. *Sales* are necessary to fuel the growth of every company. Disciplined value propositions enable *Sales* agreements between companies. *Cost Control* is a priority of every chief financial officer, along with *Accelerating Working Capital Turns, Leveraging Invested Capital,* and *Minimizing Effective Tax Rates.*

One principle that the very best businessmen and businesswomen employ is networking. The proper use of networking can enhance sales, facilitate cost control, and significantly contribute to the other drivers of shareholder value.

The Value of Networking & Relationships

No matter what company, industry, or country, people do business with people. Today in the 21st Century, many basic global industries such as auto, steel, and electronics are suffering from global supply far exceeding global demand. The purchasing buyers in the large global companies have many options for every item they procure. In addition, many of these large global companies have been through restructurings. As such, they are looking for products and services that are both competitive in price and work within their business structures and systems.

Executives in large global companies do not have the time necessary to research every company wanting to do business with them. As an accelerator in their decisions, they will rely on a group of select individuals that they know to provide these products and services or introductions to trusted people that can provide them.

In many countries, there are significant complexities—legal, financial, political and cultural—that must be addressed in order to do business. These complexities can be daunting to someone from another country trying to do business in that country. Leveraging one's network can help simplify many of these complexities and compress the time to a meaningful business relationship.

Relationships, Trust, and Integrity

Relationships between people are developed over time. Long-standing relationships result from a base of trust. This trust is two-fold: personal and professional. The personal trust is built over time as individuals help one another in a balanced manner. The professional trust is built through performance and the referrals of people that can perform. A common denominator of trust—both personal and professional—is integrity.

The use of networking allows executives to tap into these trusted relationships. Included in these trusted relationships are people who can perform and help drive business with the people they know. When given the choice, people will work with people they know and trust. It is not a coincidence that the very best executives practice networking.

Vision on the N Factor in India

By Mohan Ramani

In India, the first lessons in networking are learned through the process of understanding family relationships. These relationships are often complex and involve multiple degrees of separation. While they may seem highly attenuated, and therefore weak to Western eyes, these relationships are often invaluable for an Indian in almost every facet of his life – his education, his employment and even his choice of a spouse.

As a result, it is not surprising to note that an Indian executive's professional network often begins with his extended family. The natural next step is to network with others in his community – which can be defined in a number of ways. It could be religion such as the Jains, a particular regional origin such as the Marwaris who originally came from the district of Marwar, a caste affiliation such as the Chettiars of Tamil Nadu, or other such characteristics. One of the interesting outcomes of such a networking process is the eventual concentration of each of these communities within a single industry. For example, the Marwaris became the primary community of traders in post-Independence India while the Jains are very involved in all parts of the diamond business.

As India evolves, the networking opportunities available to young Indian professionals increase. In the last 3 decades, being a part of the alumni network of certain leading Indian educational institutions has opened a new world of relationships. This is particularly true of the professional schools such as the Indian Institutes of Technology or the Indian Institutes of Management. Graduates of these institutions are now well represented amongst the ranks of senior executives at major corporations the world over. Alumni of these schools feel very connected to others who went through the same academic experience and are very willing to help each other.

While professional networking groups in India are a relatively recent phenomenon, they are growing. It is worth mentioning the evolution of one organization in particular – The Indus Entrepreneurs (TIE). Started in the Silicon Valley by a small group of Indian entrepreneurs who had achieved great success in their adopted country, TIE is focused on helping foster entrepreneurship in all of the communities within which operates. TIE has grown into a truly global organization, with over forty chapters worldwide. They range from the Valley to Austin, TX, London, Bombay and Sydney. TIE chapters in India are very active and seem to enjoy a growing and vibrant membership. TIE chapters provide education and mentoring, in addition to opportunities for networking.

Over a decade ago, Joel Kotkin identified specific traits that helped certain diasporic ethnic groups – Jews, Indians, Chinese and several others – be successful globally in areas such as technology, communication, and business in general. In his book, *Tribes*, Kotkin predicted that these global "tribes" would have an increasing impact as the importance of national boundaries decreased in a rapidly globalizing international marketplace. The India diaspora appears to have taken this message to heart. Its members are constantly looking for ways in which to expand their network of relationships so that they can leverage their virtual global presence. This allows them access to global markets at relatively lower rates of investment, as well as a global supply chain.

Combined with this natural tendency toward extended familial networks and the growing success of the diasporic Indian community, there is a greater understanding among the emerging entrepreneurs and executives of the value of networking. These emerging leaders will work harder at developing and nurturing their networks than their predecessors. They will look to establish truly global networks, and they will look to expand their networks beyond the realm of commerce and industry to include leaders in other fields that range from the arts to politics.

Vision on the N Factor in The Netherlands

By Mitra van Raalten, MBA

Networking and interconnecting in the world of today; go back to your roots!

I have been a lucky girl; since I was twenty-five, I travelled the world and made a lot of business contacts. Getting acquainted with all these people stimulated my natural interest; my personal fulfilment of life; meeting people and discovering what people drive, makes them move and interconnect. In that period of time, neither mobile telephone nor Internet existed. One-to-one communication was essential and the basis for all possible business deals and friendships. The standard procedure to a "follow up of a sales call" after a nice encounter at a fair, a congress or business meeting was based on writing a letter (later on a fax and nowadays e-mail) or blocking my agenda a whole afternoon calling all the people I met. Why? To encounter and say thanks by voice and tone of voice for the experience shared; to relive the vivid moment, which made the difference; to express sincere interest; to stay in touch and deliver what I promised, whatever that was. Now looking back in time I realize that when technical facilities developed—first proposed as a kind of facility prolongation and mutual ways to interconnect—personal contact moments faded at that instant. Bit by bit they disappeared. We became shallow. We could hide ourselves behind the façade of technology.

Today I see people around me running from business session to business session or in the evenings and weekend days running from social encounter to social encounter... and in between the promise: I'll call you! Some do call; only a few unfortunately. Some call too late and some do not call at all. And it is so simple to deliver what you promise. Many of them hide between a quick e-mail note stating, "I know I promised to call but I have been extremely busy. I will call you soon." During a certain period of my life I was one of them. I do not look back at myself as being a nice truthful person back then.

The Experience Economy

Just as in black and white movies, where you see the family gathered around the chimney, at an old fashioned tennis club or around the pear tree on summer evenings, I feel that we should get back to these basics of showing real interest, and having a face to face conversation (you can leave the pear tree at home). Just relax and enjoy the contacts you have and the new ones you are making! It really does help when you do this in a business environment. The saying "You get out, what you put in" is very true. This is the investment any human being should continuously make. By all means, go to a networking gathering but do it the right way; return with some qualitative contacts instead of 100 business cards with names and huge titles on it but not a single story behind it. The personal contact element is essential; it gives content and volume to interpersonal relationships on the business and on the private side. It is part of today's Experience Economy. The following statement of Joseph B. Pine and James Gilmore is exactly what I would like to use as an example.

"Goods and services are no longer enough. To be successful in today's increasingly competitive environment companies must learn to *stage experiences* for each one of their individual customers. We have entered the Experience Economy; a new economic era in businesses must orchestrate memorable events for their customers that engage each one of them in an inherently personal way.

Experiences are memorable events that engage individuals in an inherently personal way, while services are mundane and mass-produced on demand. Experiences are built on top of services in the same way that services are built on top of goods. A service becomes an experience when it is personalized because customizing a service makes it memorable. The value that is created by an experience is the person's internal reaction.

The Experience Economy and the role experiences play in building a stronger, more personal relationship with employees, corporate customers, and consumers is exciting. Businesses today must deliver emotional, authentic experiences to build and encourage sustainable growth for survival in the future."

A person is looking for a real-real moment.

A moment that says what is (real) and a moment which is true to itself (real).

Networking

So let us get back to those authentic, purely personal moments and (re)start communicating with each other. But how can anyone, in the mass communication and some-times even disorder of today, distinguish the same commu-nity; people with the same need, same intention, same set of goals, same qualifications and same intentions?

Also as it comes to networking we have to keep in mind that there are two kinds of relations: relations with "strong" ties (family, relatives, and friends) and relations with "weak" ties. People within the community of "strong" ties trust each other; contacts and information are shared among them. This is purely experience driven. The disadvantage is that herewith new information and new perspectives and possi-ble growth of development will not get out of this commu-nity. Relations of "weak" ties will perhaps last a shorter time and will have a lower frequency but create an enormous input of information, advice, and knowledge outside the social network. When it comes to business relationships and networking, can we say that "weak" ties are fundamen-tally present? And how do you create a new community where you purposely add the elements of "strong" ties, so that for instance trust will be a motivational driver for both parties?

Back to the roots

Technology, to start with, seemed to have the capacity for overtaking personal contact moments one has. However, it now appears that networking – the N Factor – will continue to bring us in contact with one another, assisted by this very same technology.

However useful it is and has proven to be, technology can never enable us to get back to the strong business relationships and intense friendships. This can only be done by one's personal activity and involvement.

For me it is the mixture of both technology and human input, which creates the ideal situation and teaches us to stand with both feet on this earth; staying close to ourselves. With a little assistance from a nice piece of technology you can get back to the essence of personal, communication and interaction with the right community.

I sincerely believe that in the world of today we can be more relaxed and easier to live with and work with when fun and passion is part of our daily life; the value added balance with regard to all social aspects.

Conclusion

Globalization is the name of the game; the world is moving faster and faster. As such whether you are a High Potential or Starting Entrepreneur, it will become an ever increasing challenge to be personal to your network. Even though technological tools will consolidate into more integrated systems, the personal touch will continue to be of key importance for the strength and value of your relationship.

New methods of personal contact will develop, for instance by organizing a special event for each continent at a very high level, where you might gather people not for an afternoon but a few days.

Tools such as Podcasting, Webcasting, and Web conferencing will undoubtedly grow in importance as the quality of the visual aspect improves. You have to see people not just speak to them or have written contact. With VOIP we are on the path to making this work better than it is working today.

CONCLUSION

All of these new technology tools and techniques will require new rules of communication.

Index

Index

Skype, *see* communication
sports, *see* events
Szabo, Zsolt, 92, *see also* politics

T

Thatcher, Margaret, 129
technology,
       and communications, 53
       key role of, 9
       modern, 23, 103
Tribes, 137

U

Uchida, Mitsuyo, 123
Unilever, 2

Y

Yahoo, 57, 71
       Yahoos!'s IM, 71

THIS BOOK DOESN'T STOP
AT THE LAST PAGE!

We want to hear from you!

Join our email list to continue your experience.

WBusiness Books is not just a business book publisher, it's a community for business readers who learn and share their experiences.

Sign up for our mailing list at **www.Wbusinessbooks.com** and join the WBusiness Community.